THE PROMPT BIBLE

Founder's Edition

Understand AI. Master the Process. Create Anything.

Domenic Bianchi

Imagination Station Publishing

FOUNDER'S EDITION | VERSION 0.13

Dedication

Dedicated to every person who has looked at artificial intelligence and thought, "I know this can help me - I just need someone to explain it in a way that makes sense."

May these pages replace confusion with curiosity, help you create with more confidence, and remind you that you do not need to be a technical expert to work intelligently with AI.

A Promise to Our Readers

AI changes quickly. New tools appear, old features disappear, and today's breakthrough can become tomorrow's basic feature.

This book will not ask you to memorize every model, button, or trend. Instead, it will teach you the skills that travel with you: how to explain what you want, provide useful context, guide the work, evaluate the result, verify what matters, and improve what does not work.

Whenever a technical idea is important, we will explain it in everyday language first. Whenever a method is useful, we will show you why it matters, give you a practical example, and help you try it yourself.

A Note About Access, Plans & Privacy

Many AI services offer both free and paid levels. Free access is enough for many of the learning exercises in this book. Paid levels may provide higher usage limits, additional models or tools, larger file allowances, or other expanded capabilities.

Plans, features, limits, and availability change often and can differ by provider, device, region, or account. For that reason, The Prompt Bible does not list subscription prices or assume that every reader has access to the same features. If an exercise mentions a feature you do not have, use the closest available option and keep practicing the underlying skill.

Before uploading private, confidential, personal, client, student, business, medical, or other sensitive third-party material, review the provider's current privacy and data-use terms and make sure you have permission to use the material.

You do not need a paid plan to begin. Upgrade because you need a specific capability - not because paying automatically makes you better at AI.

The Purpose of This Book

The Prompt Bible is a practical guide to working with AI - not simply a collection of copy-and-paste prompts. It is designed to help beginners become comfortable, experienced users become more systematic, and creators turn good results into repeatable workflows.

The goal is simple: understand the technology well enough to use it wisely, master the process well enough to stay in control, and create results that are useful to you.

The Philosophy

You cannot memorize AI because AI keeps changing. What you can master is how to work with it.

Learn the principles before the products. Learn how to ask, show, guide, check, refine, and decide. Those skills remain useful even when the tool in front of you changes.

The Four Pillars

UNDERSTAND	Know what AI can do, what it cannot do, and why context matters.
COMMUNICATE	Turn your intention into clear instructions, examples, and useful source material.
CREATE	Use AI to write, research, design, plan, analyze, and build meaningful work.
IMPROVE	Question results, verify important claims, refine weak output, and save what works.

The Golden Rule

NEVER HAND OVER YOUR JUDGMENT.
Use AI to strengthen your thinking - not replace it.

Founder's Edition Roadmap

This edition concentrates on the core references, workflows, and practice systems developed for the Founder's Edition.

The technology will change. The skills you learn here should travel with you.

PART II

PROMPT ENGINEERING

Featured Reference Chapter

ChatGPT Shorthand Command Language

A practical user-defined prompt language for faster, clearer, more consistent AI instructions.

A KEY DISTINCTION

These shorthand commands are not hidden or native ChatGPT slash commands. They are compact prompt instructions whose meaning is explicitly defined by the user.

THE PROMPT BIBLE

ChatGPT Shorthand Command Language

PROMPT ENGINEERING MASTER REFERENCE

A user-defined prompt shorthand system for faster, clearer, more consistent AI instructions

IMPORTANT: These are not hidden or native ChatGPT slash commands.

They are a practical shorthand language you define and use as compact prompt instructions. Their power comes from the meaning you assign to each command and the clarity of the surrounding request.

580 core commands | 45 modifiers | 30 ready-to-use command stacks

Quick Start: How the System Works

A shorthand command is simply a compact instruction. Stack several commands before your request to describe the role, depth, tone, format, and quality standard you want.

```
/human /warm /shorten /proofread
Rewrite this announcement: [PASTE TEXT]
```

Interpretation: Make it natural + warm + shorter + mechanically correct.

Four Rules to Remember

- Commands are user-defined shorthand, not magic switches. The slash is simply an easy visual convention.
- Commands can be stacked. When several are compatible, apply all of them.
- If commands conflict, the more specific or later instruction should usually win. Example: /brief followed by /W500 is contradictory, so clarify or obey the explicit word target.
- The shorthand works best when the actual request still contains enough context: audience, purpose, source material, constraints, and desired outcome.

A Practical Activation Prompt

PROMPT BIBLE SHORTHAND MODE: When I begin a request with slash commands, treat them as compact instructions according to the definitions I provide or their clear ordinary meaning. Apply compatible commands together. If a command is genuinely ambiguous, ask what I mean rather than inventing a hidden function. Specific instructions in the request override shorthand when they conflict.

Practical note: You do not need to paste this activation prompt every time in a conversation where the shorthand has already been established. For persistent use across chats, save a selected command legend in whatever instruction/personalization feature you use, or keep this reference handy and define uncommon commands when needed.

Why This Structure Works

The system formalizes widely recommended prompting habits: be clear and specific, provide enough context, state the desired outcome or format, and refine instructions when needed. OpenAI Help Center guidance on prompt engineering and Custom Instructions supports those underlying principles. This reference turns them into memorable shorthand rather than presenting the shorthand itself as an OpenAI feature.

Section Map

1. Core Response Controls

25 commands in this section. Use one command alone or combine it with commands from other sections.

Command	What it tells ChatGPT to do
`/answer`	Give a direct answer to the request without unnecessary setup.
`/brief`	Keep the response as short as possible while still being useful.
`/concise`	Use compact wording and remove nonessential detail.
`/detailed`	Provide a thorough explanation with useful supporting detail.
`/deep`	Go beyond the surface answer and explore implications, causes, and nuances.
`/simple`	Use plain, easy-to-understand language.
`/beginner`	Assume little or no prior knowledge and explain foundational ideas.
`/intermediate`	Assume basic familiarity and skip the most elementary material.
`/advanced`	Assume strong subject knowledge and focus on higher-level detail.
`/expert`	Answer from a specialist-level perspective using appropriate depth.
`/direct`	Get immediately to the point and avoid long introductions.
`/focus`	Stay tightly centered on the requested subject and avoid tangents.
`/complete`	Cover all important parts of the request before finishing.
`/essentials`	Return only the information needed to act or decide.
`/context`	Add background information needed to understand the answer.
`/why`	Emphasize the reasons, causes, or rationale behind the answer.
`/how`	Emphasize method, process, or implementation.
`/what`	Emphasize definition, meaning, or description.
`/when`	Emphasize timing, conditions, or appropriate circumstances.
`/where`	Emphasize location, placement, or where something can be found.
`/quickstart`	Give the minimum steps needed to begin immediately.
`/overview`	Provide a high-level map of the subject before details.
`/bottomline`	End with the single most important conclusion or recommendation.
`/snapshot`	Give a compact status-style summary at a glance.
`/onepage`	Compress the answer so it could reasonably fit on one reference page.

2. Tone, Voice & Style

30 commands in this section. Use one command alone or combine it with commands from other sections.

Command	What it tells ChatGPT to do
`/human`	Use natural, human-like phrasing and sentence rhythm.
`/humanize`	Remove stiff, formulaic, repetitive, or overly synthetic wording.
`/natural`	Favor everyday sentence construction and believable word choice.
`/voice`	Preserve the writer's original personality, cadence, and intent.
`/conversational`	Write as if speaking naturally to another person.
`/warm`	Use a friendly, personable, welcoming tone.
`/friendly`	Make the language approachable and easygoing.
`/casual`	Use informal everyday language without becoming sloppy.
`/professional`	Use polished, competent, workplace-appropriate language.
`/formal`	Use a more traditional, structured, formal register.
`/confident`	Sound assured and clear without being arrogant.
`/gentle`	Soften wording and avoid harsh or abrupt phrasing.
`/empathetic`	Acknowledge feelings or perspective with appropriate sensitivity.
`/enthusiastic`	Add appropriate energy and excitement.
`/fun`	Make the writing playful and lively.
`/humorous`	Add suitable humor while preserving the purpose.
`/witty`	Use light cleverness or wordplay when appropriate.
`/serious`	Use a sober, focused tone and remove playfulness.
`/neutral`	Use even-handed wording with minimal emotional coloring.
`/respectful`	Ensure tactful, considerate wording throughout.
`/persuasive`	Write to encourage agreement or action using clear reasoning.
`/reassuring`	Use calm language that reduces uncertainty without making unsupported promises.
`/energetic`	Increase pace and momentum through active language.
`/elegant`	Use polished, graceful wording without becoming ornate.
`/plainspoken`	Use direct everyday vocabulary and uncomplicated phrasing.
`/storylike`	Use a narrative flow rather than a purely informational structure.
`/authoritative`	Use clear, decisive expert-style language while remaining accurate.

Command	What it tells ChatGPT to do
`/nocliches`	Avoid clichés, stock phrases, and tired expressions.
`/nojargon`	Avoid unnecessary technical terminology or explain it plainly.
`/noai`	Avoid stereotypical AI-style phrasing such as repetitive transitions, filler, and generic conclusions.

3. Writing, Rewriting & Editing

35 commands in this section. Use one command alone or combine it with commands from other sections.

Command	What it tells ChatGPT to do
`/write`	Create new written material from the supplied goal and context.
`/rewrite`	Rewrite existing material while preserving its core meaning.
`/improve`	Strengthen the supplied writing overall.
`/polish`	Give the text a professional final refinement.
`/proofread`	Correct spelling, punctuation, grammar, capitalization, and obvious mechanical errors.
`/edit`	Perform a broader editorial improvement of the text.
`/copyedit`	Improve grammar, syntax, consistency, usage, and style at the copy level.
`/lineedit`	Improve sentence-level clarity, rhythm, precision, and wording.
`/developmentaledit`	Evaluate big-picture structure, organization, pacing, logic, and content gaps.
`/grammar`	Focus specifically on grammatical correctness.
`/spelling`	Focus specifically on spelling and typographical errors.
`/punctuation`	Review and correct punctuation.
`/clarify`	Make confusing or ambiguous writing easier to understand.
`/simplify`	Reduce complexity while preserving the essential meaning.
`/shorten`	Reduce length without losing important information.
`/condense`	Compress the material substantially into a tighter form.
`/expand`	Add useful detail, examples, or explanation.
`/elaborate`	Develop existing ideas more fully without changing direction.
`/stronger`	Replace weak wording with clearer, more impactful language.
`/flow`	Improve transitions, rhythm, and the progression between ideas.
`/structure`	Reorganize material into a clearer logical order.
`/transitions`	Improve connections between sentences, paragraphs, or sections.
`/opening`	Create or strengthen the opening portion.
`/ending`	Create or strengthen the conclusion.
`/headline`	Generate a strong headline for the material.
`/title`	Generate suitable title options.
`/subtitle`	Generate subtitle options that complement the main title.

Command	What it tells ChatGPT to do
`/tagline`	Create short memorable taglines or positioning lines.
`/outline`	Create a structured outline before drafting or revising.
`/paragraphize`	Break dense text into readable paragraphs.
`/tighten`	Remove redundancy, filler, and unnecessary words.
`/activevoice`	Prefer clear active constructions where they improve readability.
`/rhythm`	Vary sentence length and cadence for smoother reading.
`/consistencyedit`	Standardize terminology, capitalization, names, and style choices.
`/publishready`	Refine the material to a final publication-ready standard.

4. Teaching, Learning & Explanation

25 commands in this section. Use one command alone or combine it with commands from other sections.

Command	What it tells ChatGPT to do
`/teacher`	Explain the subject like an experienced teacher.
`/tutor`	Guide the learner through the subject interactively and progressively.
`/coach`	Guide improvement through practical advice and feedback.
`/lesson`	Organize the material as a teachable lesson.
`/tutorial`	Create practical instructions that teach by doing.
`/stepbystep`	Break the process into numbered sequential steps.
`/walkthrough`	Guide the user through the complete process from beginning to end.
`/eli5`	Explain the core idea in language simple enough for a young child.
`/analogy`	Use a relatable comparison to make the concept easier to understand.
`/example`	Include at least one practical example.
`/examples3`	Provide exactly three useful examples.
`/demonstrate`	Show the concept in action rather than only describing it.
`/practice`	Create practice opportunities for the skill or concept.
`/exercise`	Generate a focused exercise based on the material.
`/quiz`	Create questions that test understanding.
`/testme`	Ask the user questions interactively to check learning.
`/answerkey`	Provide correct answers and, where useful, explanations.
`/studyguide`	Convert the material into a structured study guide.
`/flashcards`	Turn key information into question-and-answer flashcards.
`/mnemonic`	Create a memory aid or mnemonic device.
`/teachback`	Structure the explanation so the learner can restate it in their own words.
`/learningobjectives`	Create clear measurable learning objectives.
`/ageappropriate`	Adjust vocabulary, complexity, and examples for a specified age.
`/gradelevel`	Adjust material for a specified school grade.
`/checkunderstanding`	Add quick questions or checks to confirm comprehension.

5. Brainstorming & Creative Ideation

25 commands in this section. Use one command alone or combine it with commands from other sections.

Command	What it tells ChatGPT to do
`/brainstorm`	Generate a broad range of ideas before narrowing them down.
`/ideas`	Generate practical ideas around the supplied topic.
`/creative`	Prioritize originality and imaginative thinking.
`/wildcard`	Include unconventional or surprising options.
`/original`	Avoid obvious, generic, or derivative ideas.
`/fresh`	Look for newer angles or less-used approaches.
`/variations`	Produce multiple distinct versions of the same core idea.
`/alternatives`	Generate different approaches to the same goal.
`/possibilities`	Explore options without prematurely choosing one.
`/inspire`	Generate inspiration and directions rather than a finished deliverable.
`/whatif`	Explore hypothetical scenarios and their implications.
`/remix`	Recombine an existing idea into a meaningfully different version.
`/combine`	Merge two or more ideas into one coherent concept.
`/expandidea`	Turn a small idea into a fuller concept or project.
`/twist`	Add an unexpected but relevant element.
`/angles`	Find multiple ways to approach or frame the same topic.
`/themes`	Generate thematic directions around a subject.
`/concepts`	Develop higher-level creative concepts.
`/names`	Generate names for a product, project, character, brand, or feature.
`/naming`	Generate names and explain the reasoning or positioning behind each.
`/metaphors`	Generate useful metaphors for the concept.
`/promptspark`	Turn a vague idea into several stronger starting prompts.
`/unexpected`	Deliberately include less predictable ideas alongside safe ones.
`/mashup`	Blend ideas from different domains to create something new.
`/creativeconstraints`	Use deliberate limits to stimulate more focused creativity.

6. Critical Thinking & Analysis

30 commands in this section. Use one command alone or combine it with commands from other sections.

Command	What it tells ChatGPT to do
`/analyze`	Examine the subject carefully and break it into meaningful parts.
`/critic`	Identify weaknesses, flaws, and areas for improvement.
`/challenge`	Question assumptions rather than automatically accepting them.
`/devilsadvocate`	Argue against the idea to test how well it holds up.
`/skeptic`	Examine claims with healthy skepticism and demand support.
`/assumptions`	Identify assumptions that the reasoning depends on.
`/bias`	Look for potential bias in framing, evidence, or interpretation.
`/risks`	Identify plausible risks and negative consequences.
`/weaknesses`	List the weakest parts of an idea, plan, or argument.
`/strengths`	Identify the strongest parts worth preserving or emphasizing.
`/proscons`	Compare advantages and disadvantages.
`/tradeoffs`	Explain what is gained and lost between options.
`/missing`	Identify important elements that appear to be absent.
`/blindspots`	Look for overlooked issues or perspectives.
`/gaps`	Identify missing information or breaks in reasoning.
`/contradictions`	Find internal inconsistencies or conflicting claims.
`/logic`	Evaluate the quality and structure of the reasoning.
`/stresstest`	Test whether the idea survives difficult scenarios or objections.
`/counterargument`	Develop the strongest reasonable argument against the position.
`/secondopinion`	Reconsider the issue independently from another angle.
`/redteam`	Actively search for ways a plan or assumption might fail.
`/rethink`	Start over conceptually instead of being anchored to the existing approach.
`/reframe`	Describe the same issue from a different useful perspective.
`/diagnose`	Identify the most likely causes of a problem.
`/rootcause`	Search for the underlying cause rather than treating symptoms.
`/evidencegap`	Identify where claims exceed the available evidence.
`/failuremodes`	List realistic ways a plan, process, or product could fail.

Command	What it tells ChatGPT to do
`/edgecases`	Look for unusual cases that may break the normal solution.
`/premortem`	Assume the project failed and work backward to identify likely reasons.
`/postmortem`	Analyze what happened after an outcome to extract lessons.

7. Decisions, Planning & Strategy

25 commands in this section. Use one command alone or combine it with commands from other sections.

Command	What it tells ChatGPT to do
`/strategy`	Develop a longer-term approach toward the goal.
`/plan`	Turn the goal into an actionable plan.
`/roadmap`	Organize the plan into stages, milestones, and progression.
`/next`	Identify the single most logical next action.
`/priority`	Rank items by importance and urgency.
`/rank`	Order choices using stated criteria.
`/compare`	Compare two or more alternatives on relevant dimensions.
`/recommend`	Give a reasoned recommendation after considering trade-offs.
`/choose`	Select the best option based on the available information.
`/decision`	Structure the decision and the factors that matter.
`/score`	Score options against defined criteria.
`/matrix`	Create a decision matrix for comparing options.
`/scenario`	Explore plausible future scenarios.
`/bestcase`	Describe the most favorable realistic outcome.
`/worstcase`	Describe a plausible negative outcome and its consequences.
`/likelycase`	Describe the outcome that appears most probable.
`/shortterm`	Focus on immediate effects, costs, or benefits.
`/longterm`	Focus on future consequences and sustainability.
`/costbenefit`	Compare likely benefits against costs, effort, and risk.
`/efficiency`	Find ways to achieve the goal with less time, effort, or waste.
`/optimize`	Improve a process or plan for stronger results.
`/workflow`	Turn the task into a repeatable sequence.
`/system`	Turn repeated work into a consistent operating system.
`/fallback`	Create a practical backup plan.
`/milestones`	Define meaningful checkpoints for progress.

8. Role & Perspective Commands

20 commands in this section. Use one command alone or combine it with commands from other sections.

Command	What it tells ChatGPT to do
`/ceo`	Think from an executive or owner perspective, balancing strategy, resources, risk, and outcomes.
`/founder`	Think like a founder focused on product, market, resources, growth, and execution.
`/manager`	Focus on responsibilities, people, process, priorities, and execution.
`/consultant`	Analyze the situation and provide structured recommendations.
`/advisor`	Give reasoned guidance while explaining key considerations.
`/mentor`	Guide with emphasis on growth, learning, and practical judgment.
`/customer`	Evaluate the issue from the customer's point of view.
`/buyer`	Judge whether the offer is clear, trustworthy, and worth purchasing.
`/reader`	Evaluate content from the reader's experience.
`/parent`	Consider how a parent or caregiver may view the material.
`/child`	Consider how a child of the specified age may experience the content.
`/educator`	Evaluate content from an educational perspective.
`/publisher`	Consider publishing quality, metadata, presentation, and market fit.
`/marketer`	Think in terms of audience, positioning, messaging, and demand.
`/copywriter`	Write from a persuasive commercial-copy perspective.
`/designer`	Think in terms of visual hierarchy, clarity, consistency, and usability.
`/ux`	Evaluate ease of use, friction, navigation, and user experience.
`/support`	Respond like helpful customer support focused on resolution.
`/competitor`	Examine the situation from a competitor's perspective.
`/reviewer`	Evaluate the work as an independent reviewer would.

9. Research, Verification & Evidence

25 commands in this section. Use one command alone or combine it with commands from other sections.

Command	What it tells ChatGPT to do
`/research`	Investigate the subject in depth before answering.
`/web`	Use current web research when browsing is available and appropriate.
`/current`	Prioritize up-to-date information over older background knowledge.
`/latest`	Focus on the newest relevant developments or information.
`/verify`	Check important claims before presenting them as fact.
`/factcheck`	Evaluate factual statements for accuracy.
`/sources`	Provide or identify supporting sources.
`/citations`	Cite supporting sources where possible.
`/primarysources`	Prefer original research, official documents, or first-party sources.
`/official`	Prioritize authoritative official sources.
`/evidence`	Explain what evidence supports the conclusion.
`/facts`	Separate established facts from opinion, inference, or assumption.
`/timeline`	Organize relevant events in chronological order.
`/history`	Explain how the subject developed over time.
`/origin`	Investigate where the idea, term, event, or practice began.
`/definitions`	Define important terms clearly.
`/terminology`	Explain specialized vocabulary used in the subject.
`/comparesources`	Compare what multiple reliable sources say.
`/consensus`	Explain the strongest evidence-based mainstream view, including meaningful disagreement.
`/uncertain`	Clearly identify what remains unknown, disputed, or weakly supported.
`/sourcequality`	Assess the reliability and relevance of the available sources.
`/datecheck`	Check whether dates, versions, rules, or timelines are still current.
`/claimcheck`	Test a specific claim against reliable evidence.
`/trace`	Trace a claim or idea back toward its original source.
`/researchbrief`	Return a concise research summary with key findings and open questions.

10. Extract, Summarize & Organize Information

20 commands in this section. Use one command alone or combine it with commands from other sections.

Command	What it tells ChatGPT to do
`/extract`	Pull requested information from supplied material.
`/summarize`	Condense material while preserving the main meaning.
`/keypoints`	Extract the most important points.
`/takeaways`	Identify practical lessons or conclusions.
`/actionitems`	Extract tasks or actions that should happen next.
`/decisions`	Extract decisions that have been made.
`/openquestions`	Identify unresolved questions.
`/namesonly`	Extract names and named entities only.
`/datesonly`	Extract dates and time references only.
`/numbersonly`	Extract quantities, prices, percentages, and other numbers.
`/topics`	Identify the main topics present.
`/themescan`	Identify recurring themes or patterns.
`/categorize`	Group information into useful categories.
`/organize`	Rearrange information into a clearer structure.
`/dedupe`	Remove duplicates or near-duplicates.
`/merge`	Combine overlapping notes into one clean version.
`/chronological`	Reorder events or notes by time.
`/importance`	Reorder information from most to least important.
`/reference`	Turn the material into a reusable reference entry.
`/archive`	Format information cleanly for long-term records.

11. Business & Entrepreneurship

25 commands in this section. Use one command alone or combine it with commands from other sections.

Command	What it tells ChatGPT to do
`/business`	Analyze from a practical business perspective.
`/businessplan`	Create or improve a business plan.
`/businessmodel`	Explain or evaluate how the business creates and captures value.
`/revenue`	Identify possible revenue sources or implications.
`/pricing`	Analyze pricing options and positioning.
`/offer`	Develop or improve the customer offer.
`/value`	Clarify what value the product or service provides.
`/valueprop`	Create a concise value proposition.
`/audience`	Define or analyze the target audience.
`/customerprofile`	Build a practical ideal-customer profile.
`/painpoints`	Identify likely customer frustrations or problems.
`/needs`	Identify customer needs and desired outcomes.
`/objections`	Anticipate reasons a customer may hesitate or decline.
`/positioning`	Clarify how the offer should be positioned in the market.
`/differentiate`	Find meaningful ways to stand apart from alternatives.
`/competitors`	Compare relevant competitors or substitute solutions.
`/opportunities`	Identify realistic growth or improvement opportunities.
`/monetize`	Explore ways to generate income from an asset, audience, or idea.
`/upsell`	Identify logical higher-value follow-on offers.
`/bundle`	Suggest products or services that could be packaged together.
`/unitEconomics`	Examine revenue, costs, margin, and economics per unit or customer.
`/breakEven`	Estimate what would be required to cover costs.
`/marketfit`	Evaluate how well the offer matches a real customer need.
`/retention`	Identify ways to encourage customers to return or stay engaged.
`/scalability`	Evaluate how well the model can grow without proportional complexity or cost.

12. Marketing, Sales & Persuasion

25 commands in this section. Use one command alone or combine it with commands from other sections.

Command	What it tells ChatGPT to do
`/marketing`	Develop or evaluate marketing strategy and messaging.
`/campaign`	Create a coordinated marketing campaign.
`/promotion`	Generate promotional ideas for an offer or event.
`/salescopy`	Write copy intended to persuade a buyer.
`/benefits`	Translate features into customer benefits.
`/features`	Present the product or service features clearly.
`/hook`	Create a strong opening designed to earn attention.
`/hooks`	Generate multiple opening hooks.
`/cta`	Create a clear call to action.
`/urgency`	Add legitimate time or availability urgency without inventing scarcity.
`/trust`	Identify ways to increase credibility and buyer confidence.
`/objectionhandling`	Address common objections respectfully and persuasively.
`/testimonial`	Shape authentic testimonial material into readable copy without inventing claims.
`/launch`	Create a product or campaign launch plan.
`/funnel`	Map the customer journey from awareness to action.
`/leadmagnet`	Develop a useful free resource designed to attract the right audience.
`/emailmarketing`	Create marketing emails or a sequence.
`/newsletter`	Create newsletter content or structure.
`/brandmessage`	Clarify the central message the brand should consistently communicate.
`/positioningstatement`	Write a concise market-positioning statement.
`/pitch`	Create a short persuasive pitch.
`/elevatorpitch`	Create a brief verbal-style explanation of the offer.
`/salespage`	Structure a complete sales page.
`/conversion`	Identify improvements that could increase desired actions.
`/retarget`	Create follow-up messaging for people who showed interest but did not act.

13. Social Media & Content Creation

25 commands in this section. Use one command alone or combine it with commands from other sections.

Command	What it tells ChatGPT to do
`/social`	Create or adapt content for social media.
`/viral`	Search for high-engagement angles without relying on deceptive clickbait.
`/engagement`	Improve the content's ability to prompt meaningful audience interaction.
`/instagram`	Adapt content for Instagram.
`/facebook`	Adapt content for Facebook.
`/youtube`	Adapt content for YouTube.
`/linkedin`	Adapt content for LinkedIn.
`/tiktok`	Adapt content for TikTok-style short-form video.
`/reel`	Create a short-form Reel concept or script.
`/shorts`	Create a YouTube Shorts concept or script.
`/carousel`	Turn the topic into a multi-slide carousel.
`/caption`	Write a social-media caption.
`/hashtags`	Suggest relevant hashtags where they add value.
`/post`	Create a ready-to-post social update.
`/contentideas`	Generate future content ideas.
`/contentcalendar`	Create a practical publishing schedule.
`/repurpose`	Turn one piece of content into multiple formats.
`/discussion`	Create content designed to encourage thoughtful comments.
`/shareable`	Make content more useful or interesting to share.
`/saveable`	Make content practical enough that people may want to save it.
`/storypost`	Turn the idea into a short narrative-style post.
`/series`	Turn one topic into a multi-post content series.
`/community`	Create content that strengthens audience belonging and participation.
`/behindthescenes`	Turn process or progress into behind-the-scenes content.
`/contentaudit`	Review existing content for gaps, repetition, and opportunities.

14. SEO & Discoverability

20 commands in this section. Use one command alone or combine it with commands from other sections.

Command	What it tells ChatGPT to do
`/seo`	Improve content for search discoverability while keeping it natural.
`/keywords`	Identify relevant search terms and phrases.
`/searchintent`	Identify what a searcher is actually trying to accomplish.
`/seotitle`	Create search-friendly title options.
`/seodescription`	Create a concise search-friendly description.
`/meta`	Create or improve metadata fields.
`/slug`	Suggest a clean search-friendly URL slug.
`/longtail`	Generate more specific lower-volume search phrases.
`/questionseo`	Generate search questions people may ask around the topic.
`/semanticseo`	Suggest closely related terms and concepts that improve topical coverage.
`/optimizeseo`	Audit existing content for SEO improvements.
`/keywordgap`	Identify important search topics or terms that are missing.
`/topiccluster`	Group related topics into a structured content cluster.
`/internalLinks`	Suggest logical internal-linking opportunities.
`/searchsnippet`	Draft concise content suitable for search-result descriptions or answer-style summaries.
`/localSeo`	Adapt discoverability recommendations to a local market or location.
`/imageSeo`	Create descriptive image filenames, alt text ideas, and context for discoverability.
`/productseo`	Optimize product copy and metadata for relevant search intent.
`/bookseo`	Optimize book-related titles, descriptions, and keywords for discoverability.
`/seoAudit`	Perform a structured SEO review and prioritize fixes.

15. Books, Publishing & Storytelling

30 commands in this section. Use one command alone or combine it with commands from other sections.

Command	What it tells ChatGPT to do
`/book`	Approach the task as book development or publishing work.
`/author`	Assist from an author's perspective.
`/manuscript`	Review or develop manuscript material.
`/chapter`	Develop, review, or restructure a chapter.
`/outlinebook`	Create a complete book outline.
`/story`	Develop story material with narrative structure.
`/plot`	Develop or evaluate plot structure.
`/character`	Develop a character's traits, role, motivation, and consistency.
`/characterarc`	Plan how a character changes over the story.
`/worldbuilding`	Develop the setting, rules, history, and atmosphere of a fictional world.
`/dialogue`	Create or improve spoken dialogue.
`/pacing`	Evaluate or improve the speed and rhythm of the story.
`/continuity`	Check recurring story facts for contradictions.
`/storyconsistency`	Check names, traits, settings, timeline, and recurring details for consistency.
`/childrensbook`	Apply age-appropriate children's storytelling principles.
`/readaloud`	Optimize wording for natural spoken reading.
`/agerange`	Evaluate whether vocabulary, length, and concepts suit a target age range.
`/blurb`	Create concise promotional book copy.
`/bookdescription`	Write a fuller retail or catalog description of a book.
`/authorbio`	Create or improve an author biography.
`/synopsis`	Summarize the full story or book arc.
`/queryletter`	Structure a professional publishing query letter.
`/metadata`	Create or review publishing metadata.
`/seriesbible`	Organize recurring characters, settings, rules, and continuity for a series.
`/scenecheck`	Evaluate whether a scene has purpose, movement, and payoff.
`/storybeats`	Break a story into major narrative beats.
`/emotionalarc`	Map how emotion changes across a story or chapter.

Command	What it tells ChatGPT to do
`/readability`	Evaluate how easily the intended audience can read the text.
`/backmatter`	Develop useful end-of-book material such as activities, discussion questions, or resources.
`/booklaunch`	Create a practical launch plan for a book.

16. Education, Activities & Classroom Content

25 commands in this section. Use one command alone or combine it with commands from other sections.

Command	What it tells ChatGPT to do
`/activity`	Create an interactive learning activity.
`/worksheet`	Create printable worksheet content.
`/questions`	Generate questions appropriate to the topic and audience.
`/answers`	Generate corresponding answers.
`/rubric`	Create an assessment rubric with clear criteria.
`/lessonplan`	Create a lesson plan with objectives, activities, and assessment.
`/objectives`	Create measurable learning objectives.
`/stem`	Create STEM-oriented learning activities or explanations.
`/reading`	Create or improve reading material for learners.
`/comprehension`	Create reading-comprehension questions and activities.
`/vocabulary`	Create vocabulary instruction or practice.
`/phonics`	Create phonics-based learning material.
`/grammaractivity`	Create grammar practice or instruction.
`/matching`	Create matching exercises.
`/sequencing`	Create sequencing activities.
`/reflection`	Create reflection questions.
`/interactive`	Increase learner participation and active engagement.
`/exitTicket`	Create a short end-of-lesson understanding check.
`/homework`	Create meaningful homework with clear purpose.
`/classroomgame`	Create a game that reinforces a learning objective.
`/projectideas`	Generate project-based learning ideas.
`/differentiation`	Adapt material for varied ability levels or learning needs.
`/scaffold`	Break learning into supported stages that gradually increase independence.
`/extension`	Add a more challenging follow-up for advanced learners.
`/parentguide`	Explain an activity or concept in parent-friendly language.

17. AI Images, Illustration & Design

30 commands in this section. Use one command alone or combine it with commands from other sections.

Command	What it tells ChatGPT to do
`/imageprompt`	Turn an idea into a detailed AI image-generation prompt.
`/visualize`	Translate an abstract idea into a visual concept.
`/composition`	Specify subject placement, balance, framing, and visual hierarchy.
`/cinematic`	Add cinematic framing, lighting, atmosphere, and camera direction.
`/realistic`	Prioritize believable anatomy, materials, lighting, and proportions.
`/photorealistic`	Aim for a photographic rather than illustrative appearance.
`/illustration`	Frame the image as illustration rather than photography.
`/coloringpage`	Create a clean printable coloring-page prompt with appropriate linework.
`/characterlock`	Define visual details that must remain consistent across images.
`/stylelock`	Preserve a defined visual style across multiple outputs.
`/scene`	Build a complete visual scene with subject, setting, action, and atmosphere.
`/camera`	Specify camera angle, height, distance, or perspective.
`/lens`	Specify lens feel, field of view, or depth-of-field character.
`/lighting`	Define light source, direction, softness, time of day, and contrast.
`/mood`	Define the emotional or atmospheric quality of the image.
`/palette`	Define the intended color palette.
`/background`	Develop the environment behind the main subject.
`/foreground`	Add foreground elements that improve depth or framing.
`/depth`	Create layered foreground, midground, and background depth.
`/avoid`	List visual elements or errors that should not appear.
`/coverart`	Create a composition suitable for book, album, or product cover art.
`/poster`	Create a poster-oriented visual composition.
`/thumbnail`	Create a bold, legible thumbnail concept.
`/productimage`	Create a product-display or merchandising image concept.
`/mockup`	Create a realistic presentation or mockup concept.
`/layout`	Define a clean visual layout for text and imagery.
`/typography`	Specify type style, hierarchy, spacing, and placement.

Command	What it tells ChatGPT to do
`/negativeSpace`	Reserve uncluttered space for titles or other design elements.
`/printready`	Optimize visual instructions for print-oriented output and margins.
`/aspectratio`	Adapt composition to a specified aspect ratio.

18. Video, Audio & Storyboarding

25 commands in this section. Use one command alone or combine it with commands from other sections.

Command	What it tells ChatGPT to do
`/video`	Plan or create video content.
`/videoprompt`	Generate detailed instructions for an AI video tool.
`/storyboard`	Break the story or narration into visual scenes or panels.
`/scenes`	Divide content into meaningful visual scenes.
`/shotlist`	Create a practical list of individual shots.
`/cameramove`	Specify intentional camera movement.
`/pushin`	Use or suggest a slow camera move toward the subject.
`/pan`	Use or suggest horizontal camera movement.
`/tilt`	Use or suggest vertical camera movement.
`/tracking`	Use or suggest camera movement that follows the subject.
`/transition`	Suggest appropriate transitions between scenes.
`/timing`	Assign or evaluate durations.
`/videopacing`	Evaluate the rhythm and speed of scene changes.
`/broll`	Suggest supplementary footage or images.
`/narration`	Write or refine spoken narration.
`/voiceover`	Write or refine voiceover copy.
`/sounddesign`	Suggest ambient sounds and sound effects.
`/music`	Suggest musical mood, intensity, and placement.
`/openingsequence`	Develop the opening sequence of a video.
`/endingsequence`	Develop the closing sequence of a video.
`/audioedit`	Plan edits, trims, fades, spacing, and cleanup for audio.
`/previewclip`	Identify or design a short preview segment from a longer audio/video piece.
`/subtitlecopy`	Create concise readable subtitle text from narration.
`/visualbeats`	Match visual changes to meaningful narration beats.
`/continuityvideo`	Check that scenes, characters, props, and direction remain visually consistent.

19. Productivity, Workflows & Organization

25 commands in this section. Use one command alone or combine it with commands from other sections.

Command	What it tells ChatGPT to do
`/productivity`	Look for practical ways to work more efficiently.
`/todo`	Turn information into a task list.
`/checklist`	Create a reusable checklist.
`/schedule`	Organize tasks across dates or time blocks.
`/routine`	Create a repeatable routine.
`/systemize`	Turn an informal process into a repeatable system.
`/prioritize`	Determine what should happen first.
`/delegate`	Identify work that could reasonably be assigned to someone else.
`/automate`	Identify repetitive steps that may be suitable for automation.
`/batch`	Group similar tasks to reduce switching and repetition.
`/streamline`	Remove unnecessary steps or friction.
`/timesave`	Look specifically for ways to save time.
`/template`	Create a reusable fill-in structure.
`/sop`	Create a standard operating procedure.
`/process`	Document the task as a repeatable process.
`/tracker`	Design a simple way to track status or progress.
`/deadline`	Work backward from a target date.
`/weeklyplan`	Organize work into a practical weekly plan.
`/dailyplan`	Organize work into a practical daily plan.
`/focusblock`	Create a focused block of work with a clear outcome.
`/handoff`	Prepare clear instructions for another person to continue the task.
`/repeatable`	Convert one successful result into a reusable method.
`/minsteps`	Find the fewest reliable steps required.
`/dependency`	Identify what must happen before other work can proceed.
`/bottleneck`	Identify the step most likely to slow progress.

20. Troubleshooting & Technical Help

20 commands in this section. Use one command alone or combine it with commands from other sections.

Command	What it tells ChatGPT to do
`/troubleshoot`	Diagnose a problem systematically.
`/fix`	Focus on correcting the problem.
`/whyfailed`	Analyze why the attempted solution did not work.
`/errors`	Identify errors or likely failure points.
`/causes`	List plausible causes of the problem.
`/mostlikely`	Rank causes or fixes by probability.
`/oneatatime`	Give one troubleshooting step at a time rather than a long list.
`/reset`	Restart diagnosis without being anchored to earlier assumptions.
`/workaround`	Find an alternative path when the ideal solution is blocked.
`/test`	Create a simple test to isolate the problem.
`/verifyfix`	Explain how to confirm that the fix actually worked.
`/prevent`	Explain how to keep the problem from recurring.
`/simplestfix`	Start with the easiest plausible solution.
`/safestfix`	Prefer the lowest-risk corrective action first.
`/reproduce`	Define steps for reliably reproducing the problem.
`/compatibility`	Check for version, format, device, or platform compatibility issues.
`/settingscheck`	Review likely settings that could cause the issue.
`/filecheck`	Check likely file-format, corruption, naming, or path problems.
`/browsercheck`	Check likely browser-specific causes or fixes.
`/techplain`	Explain the technical issue in plain nontechnical language.

21. Output & Formatting

25 commands in this section. Use one command alone or combine it with commands from other sections.

Command	What it tells ChatGPT to do
`/table`	Present information in a table.
`/bullets`	Use bullet points.
`/numbered`	Use a numbered list or sequence.
`/paragraphs`	Use normal connected prose paragraphs.
`/headings`	Organize the answer with clear headings and subheadings.
`/form`	Create form-style fields or questions.
`/script`	Format the result as a script.
`/email`	Format the result as an email.
`/letter`	Format the result as a letter.
`/report`	Structure the result as a report.
`/guide`	Structure the result as a practical guide.
`/cheatsheet`	Create a compact quick-reference sheet.
`/faq`	Create frequently asked questions with answers.
`/comparison`	Use a comparison-friendly structure.
`/cards`	Structure information as separate reference cards or entries.
`/printable`	Format for clean printing and reference use.
`/copyready`	Return clean text that can be copied directly into another tool.
`/json`	Return valid JSON when suitable for the task.
`/csv`	Return comma-separated tabular data when suitable.
`/markdown`	Use Markdown formatting.
`/plainText`	Return plain text with minimal formatting.
`/sections`	Divide the response into clearly labeled sections.
`/columns`	Organize content conceptually into side-by-side categories when the output medium supports it.
`/worksheetformat`	Format content for a learner-facing worksheet.
`/referenceformat`	Format content for long-term lookup rather than narrative reading.

22. Prompt Engineering & Reusable Instructions

25 commands in this section. Use one command alone or combine it with commands from other sections.

Command	What it tells ChatGPT to do
`/prompt`	Turn an idea into a complete prompt.
`/promptengineer`	Analyze and improve an existing prompt.
`/upgradeprompt`	Add useful specificity, context, constraints, and output requirements to a simple prompt.
`/debugprompt`	Identify why a prompt may be producing weak or inconsistent results.
`/shortprompt`	Compress a long prompt without losing its essential instructions.
`/masterprompt`	Create a detailed reusable master instruction for a recurring task.
`/templateprompt`	Turn a one-off prompt into a fill-in template.
`/variables`	Identify which details should become placeholders or variables.
`/constraints`	Add explicit rules the output must follow.
`/formatprompt`	Specify the desired output structure inside the prompt.
`/role`	Choose and define a useful role or perspective for the model.
`/criteria`	Define the quality criteria the answer should satisfy.
`/fewshot`	Add concise examples that demonstrate the desired pattern.
`/iterate`	Produce a result, evaluate it, and improve it in another pass.
`/optimizeprompt`	Refine prompt wording for clarity, efficiency, and reliability.
`/reusable`	Convert instructions into a repeatable prompt that works with new inputs.
`/promptstack`	Combine multiple shorthand instructions into one structured prompt.
`/promptchain`	Split a complex task into sequential prompt stages.
`/finalprompt`	Return only the finished reusable prompt.
`/guardrails`	Add boundaries describing what should and should not be done.
`/inputfields`	Create clearly labeled placeholders for the user to fill in.
`/outputschema`	Define the exact fields or sections the response must contain.
`/selfcheck`	Instruct the model to check the result against stated requirements before finalizing.
`/fallbackprompt`	Add instructions for what to do if information is missing or uncertain.
`/promptlibrary`	Organize multiple reusable prompts into a named reference collection.

23. Quality Control & Final Review

20 commands in this section. Use one command alone or combine it with commands from other sections.

Command	What it tells ChatGPT to do
`/review`	Review the completed result and identify improvements.
`/doublecheck`	Check for overlooked mistakes or omissions.
`/finalcheck`	Perform a final quality review before presenting the result.
`/accuracy`	Focus on factual and numerical accuracy.
`/consistency`	Check for internal consistency.
`/completeness`	Check whether important elements are missing.
`/claritycheck`	Check whether anything remains confusing or ambiguous.
`/grammarcheck`	Perform a final grammar and mechanics review.
`/sourcecheck`	Confirm that sources actually support the claims attributed to them.
`/requirements`	Confirm that all explicit user requirements were followed.
`/constraintscheck`	Confirm compliance with stated limits and constraints.
`/quality`	Perform a broad quality-control pass.
`/bestversion`	Refine the current answer into the strongest practical final version.
`/readthrough`	Review the result from start to finish as a reader would.
`/usability`	Check whether the result is easy to use in practice.
`/tonecheck`	Check whether the tone matches the intended audience and purpose.
`/formatcheck`	Check whether formatting is consistent and usable.
`/dupcheck`	Check for repeated ideas, phrases, or entries.
`/logiccheck`	Check whether the reasoning follows coherently.
`/ready`	Return a clear verdict on whether the material is ready to use, plus any last fixes.

24. Modifier Codes

Modifiers act like parameters. They are especially useful when you want exact depth, length, number of options, audience level, tone, language, or output format without writing a full sentence every time.

Modifier	Meaning
`/L1`	Depth level 1: ultra-brief.
`/L2`	Depth level 2: concise.
`/L3`	Depth level 3: normal working detail.
`/L4`	Depth level 4: detailed.
`/L5`	Depth level 5: deep-dive.
`/W50`	Aim for about 50 words.
`/W100`	Aim for about 100 words.
`/W250`	Aim for about 250 words.
`/W500`	Aim for about 500 words.
`/W1000`	Aim for about 1,000 words.
`/O1`	Return one option.
`/O3`	Return exactly three options.
`/O5`	Return exactly five options.
`/O10`	Return exactly ten options.
`/O20`	Return exactly twenty options.
`/AGE3`	Target roughly age 3.
`/AGE5`	Target roughly age 5.
`/AGE8`	Target roughly age 8.
`/AGE10`	Target roughly age 10.
`/AGE13+`	Target teens and older.
`/GRADE1`	Target Grade 1.
`/GRADE3`	Target Grade 3.
`/GRADE5`	Target Grade 5.
`/GRADE8`	Target Grade 8.
`/ADULT`	Target an adult audience.
`/TONE:warm`	Use a warm tone.
`/TONE:formal`	Use a formal tone.

Modifier	Meaning
`/TONE:fun`	Use a playful tone.
`/TONE:neutral`	Use a neutral tone.
`/TONE:professional`	Use a professional tone.
`/FORMAT:table`	Return the result as a table.
`/FORMAT:steps`	Return numbered steps.
`/FORMAT:bullets`	Return bullets.
`/FORMAT:email`	Return email format.
`/FORMAT:checklist`	Return a checklist.
`/LANG:en`	Write in English.
`/LANG:fr`	Write in French.
`/LANG:it`	Write in Italian.
`/LANG:es`	Write in Spanish.
`/LANG:pt`	Write in Portuguese.
`/NOREPEAT`	Avoid repeating the same point in different words.
`/NOFLUFF`	Remove filler and nonessential commentary.
`/EXAMPLES`	Include examples.
`/SOURCES`	Include sources when factual research is involved.
`/FINALONLY`	Return only the finished deliverable, not commentary about the process.

Modifier Examples

`/teacher /simple /AGE8 /W250` Explain how volcanoes work.

`/brainstorm /creative /O10 /NOFLUFF` Ideas for a woodland activity book.

`/email /warm /professional /W100 /FINALONLY` Write a thank-you note to a customer.

`/research /current /SOURCES /FORMAT:table` Compare these three services.

25. Ready-to-Use Command Stacks

A command stack is a reusable recipe. Copy the stack, add your request, and replace placeholders as needed.

Professional Writing Stack

```
/human /voice /polish /flow /proofread /finalcheck
```

Natural, polished writing that preserves the author's voice and gets a final error check.

Fast Rewrite Stack

```
/rewrite /human /shorten /stronger /FINALONLY
```

A quick clean rewrite without extra explanation.

Publication Stack

```
/editor /copyedit /consistencyedit /publishready /finalcheck
```

A more rigorous final pass for material intended to be published.

Don't Just Agree With Me

```
/expert /critic /assumptions /blindspots /devilsadvocate /recommend
```

Challenges the idea before making a recommendation.

Research Stack

```
/research /current /official /verify /sources /uncertain /summary
```

Current, source-aware research with uncertainty clearly marked.

Decision Stack

```
/compare /tradeoffs /risks /score /recommend /bottomline
```

Compares options and ends with a clear recommendation.

Troubleshooting Stack

```
/troubleshoot /mostlikely /simplestfix /oneatatime /verifyfix
```

Starts with the most likely easy fix and avoids overwhelming you.

Beginner Tech Help

```
/techplain /beginner /stepbystep /oneatatime /example
```

Explains a technical task in plain language, one step at a time.

Creative Brainstorm Stack

```
/brainstorm /creative /wildcard /angles /variations /020
```

Produces a wide variety of conventional and unconventional ideas.

Business Critique Stack

```
/ceo /business /marketfit /risks /opportunities /recommend
```

Reviews an idea from an owner-level business perspective.

Customer Lens Stack

```
/customer /painpoints /needs /objections /trust /recommend
```

Evaluates an offer from the buyer's perspective.

Product Copy Stack

```
/copywriter /benefits /human /professional /cta /finalcheck
```

Creates persuasive product copy without losing a natural tone.

Social Post Stack

```
/social /hook /human /engagement /shareable /cta
```

Builds an engaging social post with a strong opening and natural CTA.

Carousel Stack

```
/carousel /hook /saveable /simple /010 /cta
```

Creates a clear, useful 10-slide carousel concept.

Video Story Stack

```
/storyboard /visualbeats /scenes /timing /cameramove /transition /sounddesign
```

Turns narration or story text into a visual video plan.

Image Prompt Stack

```
/imageprompt /composition /cinematic /realistic /lighting /camera /characterlock
```

Builds a richer, more consistent cinematic image prompt.

Coloring Page Stack

```
/coloringpage /ageappropriate /composition /printready /avoid /finalcheck
```

Creates cleaner printable coloring-page directions.

Children's Book Stack

```
/childrensbook /agerange /readaloud /pacing /storyconsistency /voice /finalcheck
```

Reviews a children's manuscript for age fit, read-aloud flow, pacing, and continuity.

Education Activity Stack

```
/educator /ageappropriate /interactive /activity /learningobjectives /answerkey
```

Creates an age-appropriate learning activity with clear purpose and answers.

SEO Product Stack

```
/productseo /keywords /searchintent /seotitle /seodescription /human
```

Develops search-aware product metadata without keyword stuffing.

Book Metadata Stack

```
/publisher /metadata /bookseo /keywords /bookdescription /finalcheck
```

Creates or checks key publishing and discoverability material.

Email Stack

```
/email /human /warm /concise /professional /finalcheck
```

Produces clear, friendly professional email copy.

Meeting Notes Stack

```
/extract /decisions /actionitems /openquestions /organize /reference
```

Turns messy notes into a useful action record.

Archive Stack

```
/extract /dedupe /categorize /reference /archive /finalcheck
```

Turns source material into a clean long-term reference entry.

Prompt Upgrade Stack

```
/promptengineer /role /context /constraints /outputschema /selfcheck
```

Strengthens a weak prompt by adding the elements that improve reliability.

Prompt Template Stack

```
/templateprompt /variables /inputfields /constraints /outputschema /reusable
```

Converts a one-off prompt into a reusable fill-in template.

Quick Answer Stack

```
/direct /brief /essentials /bottomline
```

Returns only the practical answer and the key conclusion.

Deep Learning Stack

```
/teacher /deep /analogy /example /practice /checkunderstanding
```

Teaches a concept thoroughly and checks understanding.

One-Page Reference Stack

```
/referenceformat /onepage /headings /bullets /NOFLUFF /finalcheck
```

Compresses a topic into a printable quick-reference page.

Universal Stack

```
/expert /context /stepbystep /example /finalcheck
```

A reliable general-purpose stack for many practical questions.

26. Build Your Own Commands

The most useful shorthand library is personal. Any repeated instruction can become a command if you define it clearly enough.

Command Design Formula

```
/shortname = one clear repeatable instruction
```

1. Choose a memorable name
Use a short word you will remember naturally.

2. Define one primary behavior
Avoid commands that try to mean five unrelated things.

3. State boundaries
If the command has important limits, include them in the definition.

4. Test it
Try the command on several different tasks and refine the definition if results vary too much.

5. Combine instead of overloading
Use stacks such as /human /brief /professional rather than creating one giant command for every combination.

Example Custom Commands

Custom command	Definition
`/mysummary`	Summarize into decisions, actions, open questions, and next step.
`/myproduct`	Create title, short description, full description, features, customer benefits, SEO title, SEO description, and tags.
`/myreview`	Review the work, list only material problems, then provide the corrected final version.
`/mytech`	Explain one step at a time in plain language and wait for the result before giving the next step.
`/mybookcheck`	Check age fit, continuity, pacing, read-aloud flow, repeated wording, and final polish.

27. Top 50 Quick Reference

If the full dictionary feels like too much at first, start with these 50. They cover most everyday prompting needs.

Command	Quick meaning
`/human`	Use natural, human-like phrasing and sentence rhythm.
`/brief`	Keep the response as short as possible while still being useful.
`/detailed`	Provide a thorough explanation with useful supporting detail.
`/simple`	Use plain, easy-to-understand language.
`/expert`	Answer from a specialist-level perspective using appropriate depth.
`/direct`	Get immediately to the point and avoid long introductions.
`/stepbystep`	Break the process into numbered sequential steps.
`/example`	Include at least one practical example.
`/rewrite`	Rewrite existing material while preserving its core meaning.
`/polish`	Give the text a professional final refinement.
`/proofread`	Correct spelling, punctuation, grammar, capitalization, and obvious mechanical errors.
`/shorten`	Reduce length without losing important information.
`/expand`	Add useful detail, examples, or explanation.
`/flow`	Improve transitions, rhythm, and the progression between ideas.
`/voice`	Preserve the writer's original personality, cadence, and intent.
`/brainstorm`	Generate a broad range of ideas before narrowing them down.
`/creative`	Prioritize originality and imaginative thinking.
`/variations`	Produce multiple distinct versions of the same core idea.
`/analyze`	Examine the subject carefully and break it into meaningful parts.
`/critic`	Identify weaknesses, flaws, and areas for improvement.
`/risks`	Identify plausible risks and negative consequences.
`/missing`	Identify important elements that appear to be absent.
`/blindspots`	Look for overlooked issues or perspectives.
`/compare`	Compare two or more alternatives on relevant dimensions.
`/recommend`	Give a reasoned recommendation after considering trade-offs.
`/strategy`	Develop a longer-term approach toward the goal.
`/plan`	Turn the goal into an actionable plan.

Command	Quick meaning
`/next`	Identify the single most logical next action.
`/research`	Investigate the subject in depth before answering.
`/current`	Prioritize up-to-date information over older background knowledge.
`/verify`	Check important claims before presenting them as fact.
`/sources`	Provide or identify supporting sources.
`/summarize`	Condense material while preserving the main meaning.
`/extract`	Pull requested information from supplied material.
`/organize`	Rearrange information into a clearer structure.
`/business`	Analyze from a practical business perspective.
`/marketing`	Develop or evaluate marketing strategy and messaging.
`/copywriter`	Write from a persuasive commercial-copy perspective.
`/social`	Create or adapt content for social media.
`/seo`	Improve content for search discoverability while keeping it natural.
`/book`	Approach the task as book development or publishing work.
`/childrensbook`	Apply age-appropriate children's storytelling principles.
`/educator`	Evaluate content from an educational perspective.
`/imageprompt`	Turn an idea into a detailed AI image-generation prompt.
`/storyboard`	Break the story or narration into visual scenes or panels.
`/workflow`	Turn the task into a repeatable sequence.
`/troubleshoot`	Diagnose a problem systematically.
`/oneatatime`	Give one troubleshooting step at a time rather than a long list.
`/promptengineer`	Analyze and improve an existing prompt.
`/finalcheck`	Perform a final quality review before presenting the result.

Final Principle

THE SLASH IS NOT THE POWER. THE DEFINITION IS.

Shorthand makes prompting faster only when the underlying instruction is clear. Good prompting still depends on context, specificity, constraints, audience, and a useful definition of success.

Foundation Sources

- OpenAI Help Center - Prompt engineering best practices for ChatGPT.
- OpenAI Help Center - Best practices for prompt engineering with the OpenAI API.
- OpenAI Help Center - ChatGPT Custom Instructions.

Framework note: This is an original user-defined shorthand framework. Product interfaces and official AI features change over time, so verify any product-specific guidance when current accuracy matters.

PART II EXPANSION

CONTEXT, EXAMPLES, ACCURACY & VERIFICATION

Five practical systems for getting stronger AI results without making prompts needlessly complicated.

The Core Idea

A weak result is not always caused by a weak prompt. Sometimes the instruction is clear, but the AI is missing background, examples, reliable source material, boundaries, or a definition of success. Before making a prompt longer, diagnose what information is actually missing.

The Prompt Bible Principle

Better instructions matter. Better context often matters more.

1. The Context Advantage

Purpose: Give AI the information it needs to produce a relevant answer instead of forcing it to guess.

The Seven-Part Context Frame

- GOAL - State the outcome you actually want.
- BACKGROUND - Explain the situation, project, or problem.
- SOURCE MATERIAL - Supply the facts, documents, data, or reference text that should ground the answer.
- EXAMPLES - Show what good looks like when style, structure, or quality matters.
- CONSTRAINTS - Define limits such as length, audience, budget, tone, format, exclusions, or deadlines.
- DESIRED OUTPUT - Specify the form of the answer: checklist, table, script, plan, explanation, draft, or other deliverable.
- VERIFY - Tell the AI what must be checked, qualified, cited, or flagged as uncertain.

Copy-Ready Template

My goal is [GOAL]. Here is the background you need: [BACKGROUND]. Use this source material as the primary basis: [SOURCE MATERIAL]. Here are examples or patterns to follow: [EXAMPLES]. Work within these constraints: [CONSTRAINTS]. Return the result as [DESIRED OUTPUT]. Before finalizing, verify [FACTS / CALCULATIONS / REQUIREMENTS] and clearly flag anything uncertain or unsupported.

Diagnostic Rule

If the AI is guessing, add context. If it misunderstands the task, improve the instruction. If it knows the task but misses the style, add examples. If facts matter, add trustworthy source material and verification.

2. The Example Ladder

Purpose: Teach the AI the pattern you want by showing examples instead of relying only on description.

Level 1 - Tell It

Use a clear instruction when the task is simple and the desired output is conventional. Example: “Write a warm 100-word product description for this children’s activity book.”

Level 2 - Show It

Provide one representative example when tone, structure, or formatting matters. Ask the AI to identify the useful characteristics without copying the wording.

Level 3 - Teach It

Provide several examples when consistency matters. Ask the AI to infer the shared pattern, state that pattern briefly, and then create a new result using the pattern rather than reproducing the examples.

Example-Safety Rule

Use examples to communicate characteristics, not to disguise copying. When source material belongs to someone else, extract general principles and create independently written output.

3. The AI Accuracy Ladder

Purpose: Escalate the quality of the information you provide before escalating the complexity of the prompt.

- 1. ASK - Start with a clear question or task.
- 2. INSTRUCT - Add the important requirements and boundaries.
- 3. CONTEXTUALIZE - Add project background and relevant history.
- 4. DEMONSTRATE - Add one or more examples when a pattern matters.
- 5. GROUND - Provide trusted documents, data, policies, research, or other source material when factual accuracy matters.
- 6. CHECK - Require uncertainty to be identified and important claims to be verified.
- 7. REFINE - Correct the weak point, retest, and preserve what worked.

Accuracy Principle

Do not keep adding adjectives to a prompt when the real problem is missing evidence.

4. The TRUST Check

Purpose: Prevent confident language from being mistaken for verified information.

- T - TRACE THE SOURCE. Identify where important information came from.
- R - REQUIRE EVIDENCE. Ask for supporting sources, calculations, or quoted source passages when appropriate.
- U - USE AUTHORITATIVE MATERIAL. Prefer reliable primary or expert sources when the stakes are meaningful.
- S - SCRUTINIZE IMPORTANT CLAIMS. Recheck names, dates, numbers, quotations, requirements, and consequential recommendations.
- T - TEST INDEPENDENTLY. Verify high-stakes or publication-critical information outside the AI response before acting on it.

Human Checkpoint

AI can organize, explain, compare, and draft. It does not remove human responsibility for decisions involving safety, law, finance, health, privacy, publishing rights, or other consequential outcomes.

5. The Prompt Improvement Loop

Purpose: Turn trial and error into a repeatable method for improving prompts.

- PROMPT - Run the best current version.
- RESULT - Examine what the AI actually produced.
- REVIEW - Compare the result with the desired outcome.
- DIAGNOSE - Identify the specific failure: missing context, unclear instruction, weak evidence, wrong format, poor example, or unrealistic expectation.
- REFINE - Change only what is needed to address the failure.
- RETEST - Run the improved version and compare results.
- SAVE THE WINNER - Convert successful wording into a reusable template, shorthand command, stack, checklist, or recipe.

Improvement Principle

Do not repeatedly solve the same prompting problem from scratch. When a prompt consistently works, turn it into a reusable asset.

How the Five Systems Work Together

CONTEXT tells the AI what it needs to know. EXAMPLES show what good looks like. THE ACCURACY LADDER determines when more grounding is needed. TRUST checks whether important information deserves confidence. THE IMPROVEMENT LOOP turns every useful result into a better reusable system.

One Combined Master Prompt

Help me complete [TASK]. First, identify the minimum context you need and ask only for information that materially affects the result. Use any source material I provide as the primary basis. If examples are provided, learn the pattern without copying their wording. State important assumptions, flag unsupported claims, and distinguish facts from recommendations. Return the result in [FORMAT] for [AUDIENCE], following [CONSTRAINTS]. Then perform a brief quality check against these success criteria: [CRITERIA]. If the result can be improved, revise it once before presenting the final version.

About These Five Systems

These five systems are original Prompt Bible teaching frameworks synthesized from broad, established practices in prompting, contextual learning, grounded generation, human verification, and iterative improvement. They are designed as durable reader tools rather than product-specific instructions.

PART II SUPPLEMENT

VIRAL 'SECRET CODES' DECODED

Community Prompt Shortcuts, Micro-Frameworks & What Actually Works

Not hidden commands. Memorable instructions.

THE BIG IDEA
Social posts often call ELI5, TLDR, HUMANIZE, TRUTHMODE, X10THINK and similar tokens 'secret ChatGPT codes.' They are not secret switches. They work only to the extent that the model can infer a useful instruction from the words. The Prompt Bible treats them as user-defined shorthand - a compact vocabulary for intent.

Why This Supplement Exists

The Prompt Bible already contains a large shorthand language. This supplement has a different job: help readers decode the flood of viral 'cheat codes' they encounter online, keep the useful patterns, merge aliases into clearer commands, and discard hype that implies capabilities the shorthand cannot guarantee.

What the Research Shows

- Current community libraries contain hundreds of prompt shortcuts and prompt templates, but many are aliases, duplicates, niche wrappers, or renamed versions of ordinary instructions.
- OpenAI prompting guidance consistently emphasizes clear tasks, useful context, desired output, constraints, and iterative refinement. That is the real mechanism behind shorthand.
- The slash character is optional. /tldr and "summarize this very briefly" can mean the same thing when the instruction is clear.
- A memorable code is valuable when it saves typing without hiding the actual intent.

The Prompt Bible Filter: KEEP, MERGE or G BIN

Decision	When to Use It	Example
KEEP	Distinct, clear, repeatable, durable, and genuinely useful.	/firstprinciples, /socratic, /feynman
MERGE / ALIAS	Useful idea, but overlaps an existing Prompt Bible command.	/deepdive -> /deep; /actas -> /role
G BIN	Vague hype, misleading guarantees, unsafe framing, or poor long-term value.	TRUTHMODE, X10THINK, jailbreak-style labels

Six Tests for Any "Secret Code"

- Clarity - Can a reader explain the instruction in one sentence?
- Distinctness - Does it add something not already covered by a clearer command?
- Repeatability - Will it behave usefully across several different tasks?
- Verifiability - Does it avoid promising truth, certainty, virality, or guaranteed quality?
- Durability - Will the idea still make sense if products, models, or interfaces change?
- Legal & ethical fit - Does it avoid deceptive, unsafe, or needlessly trademark-dependent framing?

High-Value Additions Worth Keeping

These are strong additions because they describe a recognizable method, learning level, research task, or decision process that was not already represented as clearly in the core shorthand library.

Command	Meaning	Example
/tldr	Return the shortest useful summary; preserve the main conclusion.	/tldr Summarize this report in 3 lines.
/eli10	Explain simply for roughly a 10-year-old level without becoming babyish.	/eli10 Explain compound interest.
/eli15	Explain at a teen level with moderate detail and correct terminology.	/eli15 Explain inflation.
/elicollege	Explain at introductory college depth with definitions and context.	/elicollege Explain photosynthesis.
/eliphd	Use advanced technical depth for an expert audience; define assumptions.	/eliphd Explain transformer attention.
/feynman	Teach by simple explanation, identify gaps, refine, then test understanding.	/feynman Teach me opportunity cost.
/socratic	Teach primarily through sequenced questions instead of immediately giving answers.	/socratic Help me understand fractions.
/firstprinciples	Break the problem into fundamental facts and rebuild the solution from them.	/firstprinciples Rethink this pricing model.
/steelman	Construct the strongest fair version of an opposing argument before responding.	/steelman The case against my plan.
/fivewhys	Ask "why?" repeatedly to trace a symptom toward an underlying cause.	/fivewhys Diagnose recurring late deliveries.
/decisionmatrix	Compare options against explicit weighted criteria.	/decisionmatrix Compare these three tools.
/riskanalysis	Identify risks, likelihood, impact, mitigations, and warning signs.	/riskanalysis Review this launch plan.
/mindmap	Organize a topic as a central idea with branches and sub-branches.	/mindmap Build a map of my book launch.
/studyplan	Create a staged learning plan with schedule, practice, and checkpoints.	/studyplan Learn basic Spanish in 8 weeks.
/mnemonics	Create memory aids tied to the exact material being learned.	/mnemonics Help me remember the planets.
/literaturereview	Synthesize a body of research by themes, findings, disagreements, and gaps.	/literaturereview Summarize these papers.
/comparepapers	Compare research papers on question, method, evidence, findings, and limitations.	/comparepapers Compare these three studies.
/localize	Adapt language, examples, units, references, and conventions for a target region.	/localize Adapt this page for Canada.

Useful Community Aliases to Recognize

Alias	What It Means	Prompt Bible Treatment
/deepdive	Alias for a thorough exploration.	Use Prompt Bible /deep when you want one stable name.
/actas	Alias for assigning a role or perspective.	Use /role, /expert, /teacher, /ceo, etc.
/informal	Alias for a relaxed register.	Use /casual.
/meetingnotes	Turn a transcript or notes into decisions, actions, owners, and follow-ups.	Keep as a convenient workflow alias.
/swot	Create a Strengths, Weaknesses, Opportunities, Threats analysis.	Keep when SWOT is genuinely the right framework.
/proposal	Draft a structured proposal around need, approach, scope, value, and next step.	Useful business shortcut.
/landingpage	Draft or review a landing page for message hierarchy and conversion clarity.	Useful marketing shortcut.
/casestudy	Turn evidence into situation, action, result, and lesson.	Useful publishing/marketing shortcut.
/translate	Translate while preserving meaning, tone, names, numbers, and formatting.	Use with target language and audience.
/interviewer	Ask realistic interview questions, then evaluate answers.	Useful role-play shortcut.
/debug	Diagnose a technical problem from symptoms, error messages, and code/context.	Useful technical shortcut.
/refactor	Improve code structure/readability without changing intended behavior.	Useful technical shortcut.

Codes That Sound Clever but Should Not Be Trusted

Code / Claim	Why It Is Weak	Better Instruction
TRUTHMODE	Sounds as if it can guarantee truth. No shorthand can do that.	Use /verify /sources /uncertain /claimcheck.
X10THINK	Vague promise of "10x" thinking without defining what better means.	Use /deep /firstprinciples /redteam /recommend.
JARGONIZE	Often makes writing sound impressive while reducing clarity.	Use /technical or /advanced only when the audience needs specialist language.
BYPASS-DETECTOR codes	Often promise to evade AI detectors or disguise provenance.	G BIN. Focus on authentic editing, voice, accuracy, and disclosure requirements.
JAILBREAK / DAN-style labels	Usually framed as attempts to bypass model safeguards rather than improve the task.	G BIN. Rewrite the legitimate goal directly and clearly.
Trademark-style art shortcuts	Names of studios/brands are brittle and poor long-term style definitions.	Describe visual traits: medium, era, line quality, palette, lighting, composition, mood.

PROMPT BIBLE RULE

Never let a catchy label outrank a clear instruction. If the code suggests guaranteed truth, guaranteed virality, guaranteed detection evasion, or a hidden capability, rewrite it as an ordinary request with explicit evidence, criteria, and limits.

Micro-Frameworks That Are More Valuable Than a Single Code

A good framework can be compressed into shorthand, but the framework itself is what makes the request robust.

Framework	Structure	Best Use
GFWC	Goal - Format - Warnings - Context	Fast way to make a vague task more specific.
ROLE-TASK-CONTEXT-OUTPUT-LIMITS-CHECK	Role/perspective - job - background - deliverable - boundaries - final verification	A durable full-prompt structure aligned with modern prompting guidance.
Perspective Flip	Beginner view -> expert correction -> final synthesis	Useful for teaching, assumptions, and blind spots.
Feynman Loop	Explain simply -> find gaps -> refine -> test	Turns passive explanation into active learning.
Socratic Loop	Question -> answer -> probe -> hint -> check	Builds understanding without immediately handing over the solution.
Steelman + Red Team	Best opposing case -> failure search -> balanced recommendation	Prevents easy agreement and improves decisions.
Three-Pass Rewrite	Meaning pass -> clarity pass -> final quality check	Preserves intent while improving readability and polish.
Research Triad	Source -> verify -> mark uncertainty	Separates evidence from inference and unsupported certainty.

Worked Examples

Example 1 - Learn a Difficult Concept

STACK
/feynman /analogy /example /quiz
Teach me how compound interest works. Start with a simple explanation, use one everyday analogy, show one numerical example, then give me five questions to test whether I understood it.

Why it works: the commands describe a learning sequence. The full request still supplies the topic and defines the output.

Example 2 - Make a Better Decision

STACK
/firstprinciples /decisionmatrix /redteam /recommend
I am comparing three options for [DECISION]. Identify the fundamental requirements first, score each option against explicit criteria, test the leading choice for failure modes, then recommend one option and explain the trade-offs.

Example 3 - Research Without Pretending Certainty

STACK
/literaturereview /comparepapers /verify /sources /uncertain
Use the supplied papers to identify themes, agreements, disagreements, methods, evidence quality, and unresolved questions. Separate what the sources directly support from your inference.

Example 4 - Decode a Viral Code

CLAIM
"TRUTHMODE: Tell me the absolute truth about this topic."

Prompt Bible rewrite: /verify /sources /uncertain /claimcheck
Check the major factual claims about [TOPIC]. Use current reliable sources where appropriate, distinguish established facts from disputed claims, and state what cannot be verified.

Worksheet: Secret Code Decoder

Use this whenever a Reel, carousel, post, newsletter, or prompt guide claims to reveal a "secret code."

Field	Your Notes
Code / phrase	______________________
Where I found it	______________________
What it claims to do	______________________ ______________________
Plain-English instruction behind it	______________________ ______________________
Is it official/native?	☐ Yes, verified ☐ No ☐ Unclear
Is the meaning clear?	1 2 3 4 5
Is it distinct from a command I already have?	☐ Yes ☐ No ☐ Unsure
Does it imply a guarantee it cannot make?	☐ Yes ☐ No
Long-term usefulness	1 2 3 4 5
Decision	☐ KEEP ☐ MERGE / ALIAS ☐ G BIN
Final Prompt Bible wording	______________________ ______________________

Worksheet: Build Your Own Shortcut

Design Field	Your Shortcut
Shortcut name	/____________
One clear behavior	______________________ ______________________
When to use it	______________________
What it must NOT mean	______________________
Required context	______________________
Compatible commands	______________________
Conflicting commands	______________________
Test prompt #1	______________________
Test prompt #2	______________________
Final definition	______________________ ______________________

Worksheet: Command Stack Builder

A strong stack usually needs only a few dimensions. More commands are not automatically better.

Dimension	Choice
Role / perspective	/______________________
Task / action	/______________________
Depth / thinking method	/______________________
Tone / voice	/______________________
Output format	/______________________
Quality / verification	/______________________
Audience	______________________
Constraints	______________________

My Stack

/_______________ /_______________ /_______________ /_______________ /_______________

My Full Request

____
____
____
____

What I Will Check in the Answer

- ☐ It answered the actual task.
- ☐ It used the supplied context.
- ☐ It followed the requested format.
- ☐ It did not invent unsupported facts.
- ☐ The shorthand helped instead of making the prompt harder to understand.

Worksheet: Viral Claim Reality Check

Question	Notes
Claim I saw online	____ ____
What evidence was shown?	____
Could ordinary prompting explain the result?	☐ Yes ☐ No ☐ Unsure
Does the claim promise a hidden mode or guarantee?	☐ Yes ☐ No
Can I rewrite the code as a clear sentence?	☐ Yes ☐ No
Did I test it on more than one task?	☐ Yes ☐ No

Result	☐ Useful shorthand ☐ Hype ☐ Needs more testing

Quick Reference: New Additions

Code	Meaning	Code	Meaning
/tldr	Very short summary	/eli10	Simple, balanced explanation
/eli15	Teen-level explanation	/elicollege	Intro college depth
/eliphd	Advanced technical depth	/feynman	Explain - find gaps - refine - test
/socratic	Teach with guided questions	/firstprinciples	Rebuild from fundamentals
/steelman	Strongest fair opposing case	/fivewhys	Trace root cause
/decisionmatrix	Weighted option comparison	/riskanalysis	Likelihood, impact, mitigation
/mindmap	Branching concept map	/studyplan	Staged learning plan
/mnemonics	Memory aids	/literaturereview	Synthesize research themes
/comparepapers	Compare studies	/localize	Adapt for region/culture

Research Note

This supplement treats community "secret code" lists as research material, compares their ideas against the Prompt Bible shorthand library, and keeps only concepts that add practical value. Community terminology is not presented as an official ChatGPT feature or copied wholesale.

Source categories reviewed:

- OpenAI Help Center - Prompt engineering best practices for ChatGPT.
- OpenAI Academy - Prompting and Power Prompting guidance.
- Community prompt-shortcut libraries advertising 200+ and 351+ shorthand/prompt examples.
- Community explanations of ELI5, TLDR, Humanize, Feynman-style learning, GFWC, perspective flips, and related shorthand patterns.

FINAL PRINCIPLE
The best "secret code" is the one whose meaning is obvious, useful, reusable, and honest about what it can and cannot do. The shortcut saves typing. The instruction does the work.

PART V

MARKETING & SOCIAL MEDIA

Featured Prompt Toolkit

The Instagram Growth & Audit Toolkit

7 AI prompts to audit, strengthen, and strategically improve an Instagram presence

How to Use This Toolkit

Use screenshots, captions, Reels, analytics/Insights, audience information, offers, and goals as evidence. The toolkit is designed to diagnose and improve an Instagram presence; it does not promise reach, virality, followers, or sales. AI should separate observations supported by the material from assumptions that need more data.

What to Gather

- Profile screenshot, bio, username, profile photo, highlights, and pinned posts.
- 8-15 recent posts/Reels/carousels plus captions and CTAs.
- Insights/analytics screenshots when available.
- Target audience, niche, offers, creator/business goal, and practical constraints.

Recommended Workflow

1. 1. Complete Audit
2. 2. Profile Optimization
3. 3. Content Gap Analysis
4. 4. 30-Day Strategy
5. 5. Reel Optimization
6. 6. Visitor-to-Customer Path
7. 7. Personal Brand Optimization

70-Point Instagram Health Scorecard

- Profile clarity: ___ / 10
- Audience positioning: ___ / 10
- Content mix: ___ / 10
- Reel quality: ___ / 10
- Brand consistency: ___ / 10
- Trust & community: ___ / 10
- Conversion path: ___ / 10

Use the lowest two scores to determine where to focus first. The score is a working benchmark, not an objective measure of account quality.

1. Complete Instagram Audit

WHAT IT DOES: Creates a top-to-bottom diagnostic of the account before individual fixes are made. It looks for weaknesses in positioning, profile clarity, content consistency, audience fit, engagement signals, and conversion path.

BEST INPUTS: Profile screenshot; bio; username; profile photo; highlights; pinned posts; recent Reels/carousels/posts; captions; analytics/Insights screenshots; target audience; offers; business or creator goal.

COPY-READY PROMPT

Act as an experienced Instagram growth, content, and brand strategist. I will provide screenshots and information from my Instagram account, including my profile, recent content, captions, and available Insights.

Audit the account across these areas:
1. First impression and profile clarity
2. Username, name field, bio, profile photo, highlights, and pinned posts
3. Audience positioning and what the account appears to be about
4. Reels, carousels, static posts, Stories, captions, and calls-to-action
5. Content consistency, visual consistency, and message consistency
6. Engagement signals and community-building opportunities
7. Trust signals and the visitor-to-customer path

For every issue you identify, explain WHY it matters and WHAT I should change. Separate recommendations into High Priority, Medium Priority, and Optional. Do not recommend changes merely to follow trends; preserve what is distinctive and authentic about the account.

Finish with:
- the 5 strongest things already working
- the 5 biggest growth constraints
- a prioritized 30-day action plan
- the single most important improvement to make first.

EXPECTED RESULT: A clear audit, prioritized issues, strengths worth preserving, and a practical action plan instead of a vague list of tips.

2. Profile Optimizer

WHAT IT DOES: Focuses specifically on the profile page - the few seconds in which a new visitor decides whether the account is relevant, trustworthy, and worth following.

BEST INPUTS: Current profile screenshot; current bio; desired audience; what you want to be known for; primary offer or goal; important links or calls-to-action.

COPY-READY PROMPT

Act as an Instagram profile-positioning specialist. Review the profile materials I provide and improve the account for clarity, trust, memorability, and conversion without making it sound generic.

Evaluate:
- profile photo
- username and name field
- bio
- profile positioning
- highlights
- pinned posts
- link/call-to-action
- overall first impression

First, explain what a new visitor is likely to understand in the first 5 seconds. Then identify anything confusing, weak, repetitive, missing, or off-brand.

Create 3 improved bio options:
A. Clear and professional
B. Warm and personality-led
C. Benefit-led and conversion-focused

Also recommend the best highlight categories, 3 pinned-post topics, and one clear primary call-to-action. Preserve my real voice and do not invent credentials, results, or claims.

EXPECTED RESULT: A practical rewrite of the profile, not just criticism - including bio alternatives, pinned-post strategy, highlights, and CTA.

3. Content Gap Finder

WHAT IT DOES: Finds what the account is overusing, underusing, or completely missing. This helps prevent a feed from becoming repetitive while keeping it focused on the right audience.

BEST INPUTS: Recent posts/Reels/carousels or screenshots; captions; content themes; audience; niche; business goal; any posts that performed unusually well or poorly.

COPY-READY PROMPT

Act as a content strategist and pattern analyst. Analyze the Instagram posts, Reels, carousels, captions, and performance information I provide.

Identify:
- what is working and should be repeated strategically
- what is being repeated too often
- topics or formats that appear overused
- important audience questions or needs I am not addressing
- missing content pillars
- places where the content may be losing attention
- gaps between what I post and what I ultimately want the audience to do

Group my existing content into clear themes. Estimate the balance between education, entertainment, storytelling, authority/trust, community, and promotion. Do not assume that high views automatically mean high business value.

Then create a gap-filling strategy with:
- 5 content areas to increase
- 3 areas to reduce or refresh
- 10 new content ideas
- the purpose of each idea
- the best format for each idea (Reel, carousel, Story, static post, Live, etc.)
- a suggested hook or opening angle for each

Keep all recommendations consistent with my niche, audience, voice, and long-term brand.

EXPECTED RESULT: A content map showing what to keep, what to reduce, what is missing, and exactly how to fill the gaps.

4. 30-Day Instagram Content Strategist

WHAT IT DOES: Turns the audit and content gaps into a usable month of content. The goal is a balanced plan - not a promise of virality.

BEST INPUTS: Niche; audience; content pillars; products/services; posting capacity; important dates; current account strengths; primary monthly goal.

COPY-READY PROMPT

Act as a senior Instagram content strategist. Based on my niche, audience, current content, content gaps, offers, and goals, create a practical 30-day Instagram content strategy.

Balance the plan across:
- Reels
- carousels
- Stories
- educational/value posts
- authority and trust-building content
- personal/storytelling content
- community-building content
- appropriate promotional content

For each content idea provide:
1. Day
2. Content pillar
3. Format
4. Topic
5. Hook/opening
6. Key message
7. Why the audience should care
8. Suggested call-to-action
9. Strategic purpose (reach, trust, engagement, nurture, conversion, retention, etc.)

Do not force daily posting if a lower frequency would produce better quality. Flag any ideas that can be repurposed into multiple formats. Keep the plan sustainable and aligned with my long-term brand rather than chasing every trend.

EXPECTED RESULT: A realistic 30-day calendar in which every post has a reason to exist and a role in the larger strategy.

5. Reel Optimizer

WHAT IT DOES: Analyzes individual Reels as pieces of communication: whether the opening earns attention, the middle keeps momentum, and the ending delivers value and a logical next action.

BEST INPUTS: Reel video or screenshots/transcript; caption; on-screen text; length; audio/narration; performance metrics if available; intended audience and goal.

COPY-READY PROMPT

Act as an Instagram short-form video editor and content strategist. Review each Reel I provide. Preserve my style and message, but identify where the Reel could become clearer, tighter, more useful, or more engaging.

Score each Reel from 1-10 for:
- first 1-3 seconds / hook
- visual clarity
- pacing
- storytelling or information flow
- viewer payoff/value
- on-screen text
- caption support
- call-to-action
- brand consistency
- likely retention risks

For each Reel:
1. Explain the biggest strength.
2. Explain the biggest weakness.
3. Identify any point where a viewer may lose interest or become confused.
4. Rewrite the hook.
5. Suggest a stronger scene/pacing structure.
6. Rewrite the caption if needed.
7. Suggest a more natural CTA.
8. Give one improved version that keeps my original voice and intent.

Do not exaggerate results or use clickbait that the content cannot deliver.

EXPECTED RESULT: A Reel-by-Reel diagnosis plus concrete revisions to the hook, pacing, text, caption, and CTA.

6. Visitor-to-Customer Path Audit

WHAT IT DOES: Examines what happens after someone discovers the account. It finds friction between profile visit, trust, interest, click, and purchase or inquiry.

BEST INPUTS: Profile; offers; link-in-bio destination; product/service descriptions; pinned posts; highlights; CTAs; purchase/inquiry process; target customer.

COPY-READY PROMPT

Act as a customer-journey and Instagram conversion strategist. Review the account materials, offers, profile, content, calls-to-action, and link destination I provide.

Map the current visitor journey:
Discovery -> Profile Visit -> Understanding -> Trust -> Interest -> Action -> Purchase/Inquiry -> Follow-up

At each stage identify:
- what the visitor needs to understand or feel
- what is currently helping
- what may create friction, uncertainty, or drop-off
- what trust signal is missing
- what call-to-action or next step would be clearer

Then recommend improvements to profile positioning, pinned content, highlights, calls-to-action, offer presentation, link destination, and follow-up content.

Create a simple improved visitor-to-customer path using only the steps that are actually necessary. Keep the experience authentic and low-pressure. Do not recommend manipulative scarcity, fabricated social proof, or promises that cannot be supported.

EXPECTED RESULT: A funnel map that shows exactly where visitors may be dropping off and how to create a clearer path to action.

7. Personal Brand Optimizer

WHAT IT DOES: Clarifies what the creator or business should become known for, which themes deserve more attention, and what makes the account memorable instead of interchangeable.

BEST INPUTS: Profile; recent posts; biography/background; niche; audience; values; expertise; products/services; topics you enjoy creating; content you do not want to make.

COPY-READY PROMPT

Act as a personal-brand strategist. Review the Instagram profile and content I provide and help me define a stronger, more memorable, trustworthy, and consistent brand.

Analyze:
- what I currently appear to be known for
- the strongest recurring themes in my content
- what feels distinctive or authentic
- what feels generic, inconsistent, distracting, or unnecessary
- what deserves more attention
- what I should reduce, reposition, or remove
- what my audience should remember after visiting

Then recommend:
1. A clear brand positioning statement
2. 3-5 core content pillars
3. A simple brand promise/value proposition
4. Signature topics or recurring series I could own
5. A tone/voice description
6. Visual consistency principles
7. Content boundaries - what does NOT belong
8. Five examples of posts that reinforce the brand

Preserve my personality. Do not manufacture an artificial persona simply because it may appear more marketable.

EXPECTED RESULT: A clear answer to the question: "What should this account become known for?" - with practical pillars and boundaries.

The Master Instagram Audit Prompt

Use this version for one comprehensive review. Use the seven specialist prompts when you want a slower, more focused improvement process.

MASTER COPY-READY PROMPT

Act as an experienced Instagram content, branding, audience, and conversion strategist. I will provide screenshots and information from my Instagram account, including my profile, bio, highlights, pinned posts, recent posts, Reels, carousels, Stories where available, captions, analytics/Insights, audience information, offers, and business or creator goals.

Evaluate the account across seven areas:
1. Profile clarity and first impression
2. Audience and positioning
3. Content quality, mix, and consistency
4. Reels and short-form content
5. Engagement and community building
6. Visitor-to-customer journey
7. Personal brand strength

For each area identify:
- What is working
- What is weakening the account
- What should be changed
- What should be removed, reduced, or refreshed
- What deserves more attention
- Specific next actions

Rank recommendations as High Priority, Medium Priority, or Optional. Distinguish between observations supported by the material I supplied and assumptions that require more data. Do not promise virality, follower growth, sales, or algorithmic outcomes.

Then create:
- 3 optimized bio options
- 3-5 core content pillars
- a content-gap analysis
- a sustainable 30-day content direction
- 10 Reel ideas with hooks
- 10 carousel/post ideas
- suggested calls-to-action
- an improved visitor-to-customer path
- the five changes most likely to strengthen the account

Preserve my authentic personality and brand. Do not turn the account into generic social-media content. Ask for missing information only when it materially affects the quality of the recommendation.

Prompt Bible Shorthand Stack

/instagram /audit /critic /brand /contentstrategy /reels /funnel /priority /actionplan

The shorthand commands are user-defined prompt instructions, not hidden/native ChatGPT commands.

Monthly Maintenance

What Changed?

Compare this month with last month and identify meaningful changes, separating patterns from noise.

Best Content Lessons

Analyze the strongest posts for reusable principles without simply duplicating them.

Weak Content Lessons

Analyze weak posts while clearly labeling any conclusion that cannot be confirmed.

Content Balance Check

Classify the month by content pillar and strategic purpose, then flag gaps.

Next-Month Focus

Recommend the three most important content priorities for the next month based on evidence and available capacity.

The Prompt Bible Principle

Do not ask AI to "make my Instagram grow." Give it evidence, define the goal, ask it to diagnose the account, and require prioritized actions. Better inputs make better audits; better audits make better decisions.

Platform note: This is an original expanded workflow built to teach a reusable social-media system rather than reproduce a source carousel. Platform features and algorithms change, so treat platform-specific recommendations as guidance to verify rather than permanent rules.

PART VI

AI IMAGE CREATION

Featured Video Prompt Reference

30 AI Video Visual Style Prompts

Thirty reusable visual treatments for turning one scene into dramatically different video aesthetics.

EDITORIAL NOTE

These are descriptive prompt frameworks, not hidden model commands. Exact interpretation varies by video model, so treat each as a strong starting point and refine camera, motion, lighting, duration, and continuity as needed.

How to Use This Reference

Each entry contains three things: a plain-language description of the look, suggested use cases, and a copy-ready style prompt. Replace the bracketed placeholder with your own subject or scene, then add the scene details that matter to your project.

IMPORTANT

These prompts describe visual characteristics. They are not official presets, secret codes, or guaranteed one-click styles. Different AI video systems may interpret the same wording differently.

The Master Video Prompt Formula

The style prompt works best when it is attached to a clear scene description. A useful structure is:

[SUBJECT] + [ACTION] + [SETTING] + [LIGHTING] + [CAMERA] + [STYLE PROMPT] + [CONSISTENCY RULES]

Example scene setup:

A small woodland animal walks slowly through a sunlit forest clearing. Warm late-afternoon light filters through the trees. The camera follows with a gentle low tracking shot. [INSERT ONE OF THE 30 STYLE PROMPTS]. Maintain consistent character appearance, natural motion, environmental continuity, and stable proportions. No sudden cuts, unwanted text, or distorted anatomy.

PRACTICAL RULE

Describe the scene first. Add the style second. Then add motion, camera, lighting, continuity, and exclusions. A style name by itself rarely gives enough control.

Five Controls That Matter Most

- **1. Subject & action:** Who or what is on screen, and exactly what is happening.
- **2. Camera:** Shot size, angle, lens feel, movement, and whether the camera is locked or moving.
- **3. Lighting:** Time of day, direction, softness, contrast, glow, and atmosphere.
- **4. Motion:** How quickly characters, objects, particles, fabric, foliage, or the camera should move.
- **5. Continuity:** What must remain unchanged: character appearance, clothing, proportions, materials, environment, and style.

A Useful Testing Method

Use the same short scene with several different style prompts. Keeping subject, action, camera, and lighting identical makes it much easier to see what the style itself changes. Once you choose a winner, refine only that version.

Quick Directory: All 30 Styles

Use this page when you know the look you want and only need the style number and name.

#	Video Style	Family
1	Layered Paper-Craft Diorama	Handcrafted / tactile
2	Claymation Stop-Motion	Handcrafted / tactile
3	Polished Family-Friendly 3D Animation	3D animation
4	Hand-Painted Whimsical Anime	2D illustrated animation
5	1990s Retro Cel Animation	2D illustrated animation
6	Watercolor Illustration Animation	2D illustrated animation
7	Ink-Wash / Sumi-e Inspired Animation	2D illustrated animation
8	Flat Vector Motion Illustration	Graphic / motion design
9	Isometric 3D Miniature World	3D animation
10	Retro 8-Bit Pixel Art	Retro / game
11	Comic-Book Motion Panels	Graphic / illustrated
12	Black-and-White Noir Sketch	Cinematic / illustrated
13	Chalkboard Doodle Animation	Handcrafted / educational
14	Soft Felt Puppet World	Handcrafted / tactile
15	Interlocking Brick Toy Animation	Toy / miniature
16	Origami Paper-Fold Animation	Handcrafted / tactile
17	Low-Poly 3D	3D animation
18	Soft Claymorphism 3D	3D animation
19	Cinematic Photorealism	Live-action / cinematic
20	Magical Storybook 3D Cinema	3D animation
21	Satirical Construction-Paper Cutout	2D cutout / comedy
22	Childlike Crayon Drawing	Hand-drawn / playful
23	Vintage Travel Poster Animation	Retro graphic
24	Cyberpunk Neon 3D	Cinematic / sci-fi
25	Fantasy Storybook Illustration	Illustrated / fantasy
26	Dark Whimsical Textile Stop-Motion	Handcrafted / atmospheric
27	Minimalist Line-Art Animation	Graphic / minimalist
28	Bold Sticker Animation	Graphic / social
29	Sand Animation	Handcrafted / transformative
30	Hand-Carved Wooden Figure Animation	Handcrafted / folk-art

01. Layered Paper-Craft Diorama | Handcrafted / tactile

CREATES: A miniature world of stacked, cut, and folded paper layers.

BEST FOR: Storybooks, nature, villages, education, gentle fantasy.

COPY-READY STYLE PROMPT

Create [SUBJECT / SCENE] as a layered paper-craft diorama with visible cut edges, folded surfaces, stacked depth, handmade imperfections, soft shadows, and miniature scenery. Use restrained stop-motion movement, warm lighting, tactile paper texture, and consistent paper materials throughout.

02. Claymation Stop-Motion | Handcrafted / tactile

CREATES: Characters and scenery sculpted from real modeling clay.

BEST FOR: Children, comedy, food, family stories, whimsical characters.

COPY-READY STYLE PROMPT

Transform [SUBJECT / SCENE] into handcrafted claymation with rounded forms, subtle fingerprints, tactile surfaces, miniature sets, warm studio lighting, and intentionally stepped stop-motion movement. Keep character proportions, materials, and clay texture consistent between shots.

03. Polished Family-Friendly 3D Animation | 3D animation

CREATES: High-end theatrical 3D animation with expressive characters and cinematic environments.

BEST FOR: Children's stories, fantasy, adventure, emotional storytelling.

COPY-READY STYLE PROMPT

Create [SUBJECT / SCENE] as polished family-friendly 3D animation with expressive characters, readable silhouettes, detailed environments, cinematic lighting, rich color, fluid movement, and graceful camera work. Preserve character identity and proportions throughout every frame.

04. Hand-Painted Whimsical Anime | 2D illustrated animation

CREATES: Dreamlike hand-painted animation with lush nature and poetic pacing.

BEST FOR: Nature, childhood memories, fantasy, reflective storytelling.

COPY-READY STYLE PROMPT

Render [SUBJECT / SCENE] as whimsical hand-painted animation with delicate linework, painterly backgrounds, natural scenery, soft atmospheric lighting, and understated expressive characters. Add gentle environmental motion, warm natural color, poetic pacing, and slow graceful camera movement.

05. 1990s Retro Cel Animation | 2D illustrated animation

CREATES: Nostalgic hand-drawn cel animation with bold outlines, limited shading, and vintage color.

BEST FOR: Nostalgia, urban nights, action, romance, retro storytelling.

COPY-READY STYLE PROMPT

Create [SUBJECT / SCENE] as 1990s-inspired cel animation with strong ink outlines, two- or three-tone shading, painted backgrounds, muted vintage color, expressive poses, subtle film grain, and limited-frame motion. Keep line weight, palette, and character design consistent throughout.

06. Watercolor Illustration Animation | 2D illustrated animation

CREATES: A living watercolor painting with translucent washes, pigment blooms, and paper texture.

BEST FOR: Memories, nature, children's stories, quiet emotional scenes.

COPY-READY STYLE PROMPT

Transform [SUBJECT / SCENE] into animated watercolor using translucent washes, paper grain, soft pigment blooms, irregular edges, gentle color bleeding, and layered brushwork. Use restrained subject motion, slow camera movement, soft natural light, and a consistent handmade painted appearance.

07. Ink-Wash / Sumi-e Inspired Animation | 2D illustrated animation

CREATES: Expressive ink-wash animation built around brushwork, negative space, and mist.

BEST FOR: Mountains, nature, poetry, contemplation, historical mood.

COPY-READY STYLE PROMPT

Create [SUBJECT / SCENE] with ink-wash-inspired aesthetics using expressive black brush strokes, varied ink density, textured paper, elegant negative space, restrained accent color, and misty forms. Animate fog, water, branches, and fabric slowly while preserving a minimal, meditative composition.

08. Flat Vector Motion Illustration | Graphic / motion design

CREATES: Clean modern 2D motion graphics using crisp vector shapes and simplified forms.

BEST FOR: Explainers, education, business, health, process videos.

COPY-READY STYLE PROMPT

Render [SUBJECT / SCENE] as flat-vector animation with crisp geometric shapes, bold flat color, minimal shading, simplified readable characters, and clear visual hierarchy. Use smooth 2D motion, elegant transitions, restrained camera movement, and a consistent palette without realistic textures.

09. Isometric 3D Miniature World | 3D animation

CREATES: A detailed miniature environment viewed from an elevated diagonal angle.

BEST FOR: Buildings, rooms, cities, processes, business explainers.

COPY-READY STYLE PROMPT

Create [SUBJECT / SCENE] as an isometric miniature 3D world with clean geometric construction, miniature-scale detail, soft ambient shadows, and consistent elevated perspective. Add subtle natural actions and a slow orbit, pan, or rotation without breaking the miniature-world illusion.

10. Retro 8-Bit Pixel Art | Retro / game

CREATES: Classic low-resolution pixel art with a limited palette and sprite-like motion.

BEST FOR: Games, humor, nostalgia, challenges, tutorials.

COPY-READY STYLE PROMPT

Transform [SUBJECT / SCENE] into 8-bit pixel-art animation using chunky pixel geometry, a limited palette, sprite characters, tiled environments, and frame-by-frame game-style movement. Use side-scrolling, top-down, or fixed arcade framing and keep every object aligned to the pixel grid.

11. Comic-Book Motion Panels | Graphic / illustrated

CREATES: A moving comic book using bold inks, halftones, panels, and dramatic framing.

BEST FOR: Action, heroes, humor, dramatic storytelling.

COPY-READY STYLE PROMPT

Create [SUBJECT / SCENE] as a moving comic book with bold ink outlines, halftone shading, graphic color blocks, dramatic perspective, action lines, and panel compositions. Use camera pushes, close-ups, page-like transitions, and selective motion while keeping character and ink style consistent.

12. Black-and-White Noir Sketch | Cinematic / illustrated

CREATES: Moody monochrome sketch animation with charcoal texture and hard shadows.

BEST FOR: Mystery, suspense, crime, psychological stories.

COPY-READY STYLE PROMPT

Render [SUBJECT / SCENE] as black-and-white noir illustration using graphite and charcoal texture, deep shadows, stark directional light, wet reflections, smoke or fog, and high contrast. Add subtle film grain, restrained movement, and slow detective-film camera motion.

13. Chalkboard Doodle Animation | Handcrafted / educational

CREATES: Hand-drawn chalk marks that appear, erase, and transform on a textured blackboard.

BEST FOR: Teaching, explainers, classroom content, simple processes.

COPY-READY STYLE PROMPT

Create [SUBJECT / SCENE] as animated chalk drawings on a textured blackboard. Use hand-drawn white and colored chalk, visible dust, simple diagrams, arrows, labels, and playful illustrations. Let elements draw, erase, transform, and reconnect in a clear sequence while keeping the board fixed.

14. Soft Felt Puppet World | Handcrafted / tactile

CREATES: A cozy miniature world made from felt, fabric, stitches, and soft puppet materials.

BEST FOR: Young children, bedtime stories, family scenes, cozy fantasy.

COPY-READY STYLE PROMPT

Transform [SUBJECT / SCENE] into a felt-and-fabric puppet world with visible fibers, stitched seams, embroidered details, soft stuffing, textile clothing, and miniature scenery. Use gentle puppet-like motion, warm theatrical lighting, and shallow depth of field to emphasize tactile texture and cozy scale.

15. Interlocking Brick Toy Animation | Toy / miniature

CREATES: A complete world constructed from colorful modular plastic bricks.

BEST FOR: Construction, vehicles, cities, playful education, humor.

COPY-READY STYLE PROMPT

Rebuild [SUBJECT / SCENE] from colorful interlocking toy bricks with visible connection points, modular forms, and glossy plastic surfaces. Animate construction and interaction with playful miniature timing, use macro-style cinematography, and maintain consistent brick scale throughout.

16. Origami Paper-Fold Animation | Handcrafted / tactile

CREATES: Characters and objects made from folded paper that can transform through folds.

BEST FOR: Birds, animals, nature, transformation, elegant explainers.

COPY-READY STYLE PROMPT

Transform [SUBJECT / SCENE] into origami animation using folded-paper characters, objects, and scenery with visible creases, angular planes, crisp edges, and subtle paper grain. Animate natural unfolding, refolding, and transformation while directional light emphasizes geometry and clean shadows.

17. Low-Poly 3D | 3D animation

CREATES: Stylized 3D built from visible polygon facets and simplified geometry.

BEST FOR: Landscapes, games, technology, travel, abstract explainers.

COPY-READY STYLE PROMPT

Render [SUBJECT / SCENE] as low-poly 3D animation using visible facets, simplified polygonal forms, clean lighting, attractive color blocking, minimal texture, and smooth cinematic camera movement. Keep the geometry intentional and avoid realistic skin, fur, or fine surface detail.

18. Soft Claymorphism 3D | 3D animation

CREATES: Rounded, matte 3D shapes with friendly forms and soft shadows.

BEST FOR: Education, health, organization, children's content, UI explainers.

COPY-READY STYLE PROMPT

Create [SUBJECT / SCENE] in soft claymorphism 3D with smooth rounded forms, matte tactile surfaces, inflated-looking shapes, gentle color, subtle ambient shadows, and simplified characters. Use fluid, softly elastic motion and keep the composition clean, readable, and evenly lit.

19. Cinematic Photorealism | Live-action / cinematic

CREATES: Believable live-action imagery with realistic materials, anatomy, lighting, and camera motion.

BEST FOR: Film, documentary, advertising, realistic storytelling.

COPY-READY STYLE PROMPT

Create [SUBJECT / SCENE] as cinematic photorealistic footage with realistic anatomy and materials, believable movement, natural environmental detail, film lighting, shallow depth of field, restrained color grading, and subtle atmosphere. Use a controlled dolly, tracking, or crane move and preserve continuity between frames.

20. Magical Storybook 3D Cinema | 3D animation

CREATES: Theatrical 3D with fantasy atmosphere, luminous lighting, and storybook charm.

BEST FOR: Fairy tales, children's books, fantasy adventure, magical worlds.

COPY-READY STYLE PROMPT

Render [SUBJECT / SCENE] as magical storybook 3D cinema with expressive characters, richly detailed fantasy environments, atmospheric color, practical-looking magical light, soft volumetric glow, and cinematic framing. Use polished character-driven movement, gentle camera motion, and stable visual continuity.

21. Satirical Construction-Paper Cutout | 2D cutout / comedy

CREATES: Flat paper characters with intentionally limited movement and simple graphic shapes.

BEST FOR: Comedy, satire, original parody-style content, social sketches.

COPY-READY STYLE PROMPT

Create [SUBJECT / SCENE] as satirical construction-paper cutout animation using flat geometric characters, thick outlines, simple facial features, colorful paper texture, and limited hinged movement. Use stiff comedic timing, simple graphic backgrounds, and an original look that does not copy a specific franchise.

22. Childlike Crayon Drawing | Hand-drawn / playful

CREATES: A child's crayon drawing brought to life with waxy texture and imperfect lines.

BEST FOR: Children, family memories, school content, playful storytelling.

COPY-READY STYLE PROMPT

Transform [SUBJECT / SCENE] into animated crayon art using waxy texture, uneven hand-drawn outlines, imperfect coloring, simple childlike proportions, textured paper, and cheerful color. Add playful, slightly wobbly movement while preserving the spontaneous handmade imperfections.

23. Vintage Travel Poster Animation | Retro graphic

CREATES: Mid-century poster graphics with subtle motion while preserving a printed look.

BEST FOR: Travel, landmarks, tourism, history, destination reels.

COPY-READY STYLE PROMPT

Render [SUBJECT / SCENE] as an animated mid-century travel poster with simplified shapes, a limited vintage palette, screen-print texture, softly aged paper, bold scenic composition, and retro illustration. Add subtle parallax, gentle camera movement, and minimal environmental motion while preserving the printed-poster aesthetic.

24. Cyberpunk Neon 3D | Cinematic / sci-fi

CREATES: A futuristic night world filled with neon, rain, fog, reflections, and technology.

BEST FOR: Science fiction, technology, vehicles, action, futuristic cities.

COPY-READY STYLE PROMPT

Transform [SUBJECT / SCENE] into a cyberpunk 3D night world with towering architecture, rain-soaked surfaces, vivid neon, holographic light, reflective streets, atmospheric fog, technological detail, and deep shadow. Add cinematic tracking movement, volumetric glow, realistic reflections, and controlled environmental motion.

25. Fantasy Storybook Illustration | Illustrated / fantasy

CREATES: A richly painted fantasy illustration animated with subtle motion and enchanted atmosphere.

BEST FOR: Fairy tales, children's stories, mythology, enchanted nature.

COPY-READY STYLE PROMPT

Create [SUBJECT / SCENE] as an animated fantasy storybook illustration with intricate hand-painted detail, enchanted settings, luminous magical light, textured surfaces, and whimsical character design. Animate particles, foliage, fabric, pages, and characters subtly while the camera moves gently through the illustrated world.

26. Dark Whimsical Textile Stop-Motion | Handcrafted / atmospheric

CREATES: Moody fabric-and-felt puppets in miniature sets, charming but slightly eerie.

BEST FOR: Fantasy, Halloween, mystery, atmospheric children's stories.

COPY-READY STYLE PROMPT

Create [SUBJECT / SCENE] as dark whimsical textile stop-motion with fabric-and-felt puppets, stitched details, miniature clothing, handmade imperfections, intricate sets, moody directional lighting, and rich tactile texture. Use slightly eerie but beautiful stop-motion movement and keep the original design consistent across shots.

27. Minimalist Line-Art Animation | Graphic / minimalist

CREATES: Elegant thin-line animation using negative space and continuous transformations.

BEST FOR: Explainers, artistic storytelling, sophisticated branding, concepts.

COPY-READY STYLE PROMPT

Render [SUBJECT / SCENE] as minimalist line-art animation using thin consistent lines, abundant negative space, very limited color, simplified shapes, and graceful continuous transformations. Keep motion smooth and sophisticated, every frame uncluttered, and unnecessary detail out of the composition.

28. Bold Sticker Animation | Graphic / social

CREATES: Bright sticker-like characters and objects that pop, bounce, and snap into place.

BEST FOR: Reels, children's videos, social posts, explainers, playful branding.

COPY-READY STYLE PROMPT

Transform [SUBJECT / SCENE] into bold sticker animation with thick outlines, bright flat color, clean borders, simplified expressive features, and subtle dimensional shadowing. Let characters and objects bounce, pop, slide, and snap into place with energetic motion while staying crisp and readable.

29. Sand Animation | Handcrafted / transformative

CREATES: Fine grains of sand that gather, dissolve, and reshape into new images.

BEST FOR: Transformation, storytelling, history, art, poetic sequences.

COPY-READY STYLE PROMPT

Create [SUBJECT / SCENE] as handcrafted sand animation in which grains gather, flow, dissolve, and reshape into characters, landscapes, symbols, and objects. Use warm directional lighting, visible grain texture, smooth organic transitions, and mesmerizing overhead cinematography.

30. Hand-Carved Wooden Figure Animation | Handcrafted / folk-art

CREATES: Carved wooden characters moving like articulated toys in warm miniature environments.

BEST FOR: Folk tales, history, rustic scenes, children's storytelling.

COPY-READY STYLE PROMPT

Transform [SUBJECT / SCENE] into hand-carved wooden figure animation with visible wood grain, chisel marks, carved edges, folk-art detail, and warm natural tones. Let characters move like articulated wooden toys in miniature carved environments using soft lighting, shallow depth of field, and subtle stop-motion-style movement.

Quick Style-Stacking Recipes

You can combine a primary style with a secondary treatment, but keep one clearly dominant. These examples show the idea:

Recipe	Combine These Traits
Cozy Storybook	Watercolor Illustration + warm golden-hour light + slow push-in + gentle wind movement.
Playful Children's Video	Soft Claymorphism 3D + bright clean lighting + gentle elastic motion + simple camera orbit.
Dark Fantasy	Dark Textile Stop-Motion + moonlit fog + slow dolly + restrained puppet motion.
Retro Adventure	1990s Cel Animation + dramatic sunset + side-scrolling camera + limited-frame action.
Elegant Educational	Flat Vector Motion Illustration + minimalist line art accents + fixed camera + smooth morph transitions.
Cinematic Sci-Fi	Cyberpunk Neon 3D + photorealistic materials + rain + slow tracking shot + volumetric fog.

Final Prompt Bible Principle

STYLE IS ONLY ONE LAYER

A strong video prompt combines subject, action, environment, camera, lighting, motion, visual style, and continuity. The better those layers agree with one another, the more coherent the result tends to be.

Reference note: This chapter is an original creator reference developed from a broad visual-style concept. It uses descriptive visual language rather than copying branded character styles or relying on named entertainment franchises.

PART VII

BUSINESS & AI WORKFLOWS

Featured Workflow Reference

The AI-Powered Workplace

20 practical AI workflows for creators, small businesses, educators, and professionals.

Remove busywork. Strengthen decisions. Keep humans responsible for the final result.

Why This Chapter Matters

AI is most valuable when it becomes part of a repeatable workflow instead of a one-time novelty. The goal is not to replace people with software. The goal is to reduce repetitive work, surface useful information faster, preserve institutional knowledge, and give people more time for judgment, creativity, and relationships.

This chapter builds on common workplace-AI patterns, including ideas drawn from a public Rundown AI overview, then generalizes them into an original, tool-flexible system with human checkpoints and safeguards.

Tools change quickly. Verify current features, pricing, privacy settings, permissions, and availability before building an important workflow around any product.

The Master AI Workflow Formula

A strong AI workflow usually has seven layers:

- 1. TRIGGER - What event starts the workflow?
- 2. INPUT - What information, files, conversation, or data does the AI receive?
- 3. ROLE - What specific job should the AI perform?
- 4. PROCESS - What steps should the AI follow?
- 5. HUMAN CHECKPOINT - Where must a person review, decide, approve, or edit?
- 6. OUTPUT - What finished artifact or action should result?
- 7. FEEDBACK LOOP - What should be saved so the workflow improves next time?

COPY-READY PROMPT
Act as a workflow designer. I want to improve this recurring task: [TASK]. Map it using TRIGGER, INPUT, ROLE, PROCESS, HUMAN CHECKPOINT, OUTPUT, and FEEDBACK LOOP. Identify what should be automated, what should remain human-controlled, what information is required, and the simplest version I can test first.

Quick Directory: 20 Practical AI Workflows

- 1. Meeting Capture & Action Assistant
- 2. Scheduling & Calendar Coordination Agent
- 3. Avatar-Assisted Content Production
- 4. Recruiting & Onboarding Knowledge Assistant
- 5. Research & Video Learning Assistant
- 6. Multi-Model Code Review & Debugging
- 7. Business Operations Analyst
- 8. On-Brand Design Pipeline
- 9. Human-in-the-Loop Customer Support
- 10. Voice-to-Content Idea Pipeline
- 11. Email Triage & Reply Drafting
- 12. Document & Policy Analysis
- 13. Content Repurposing Engine
- 14. Publishing & Metadata Assistant
- 15. Product Listing & Storefront Assistant
- 16. Social Content Planning System
- 17. Public Market & Competitor Research
- 18. Project Planning & Task Breakdown
- 19. Quality-Control / Preflight Reviewer
- 20. Personal Knowledge Base & Creator Archive

1. Meeting Capture & Action Assistant

Purpose: Turn meetings into usable records: summaries, decisions, owners, deadlines, unresolved questions, and next steps.

Best for: Team meetings, client calls, interviews, planning sessions, school meetings, creative reviews.

Workflow

- Capture or transcribe the meeting with permission.
- Ask AI to separate decisions, action items, risks, questions, and follow-ups.
- Assign owners and dates only when they are explicitly stated; flag anything ambiguous.
- Have a human review the summary before it is shared.
- Store the approved notes in the team workspace so future meetings can refer back to them.

COPY-READY PROMPT
Using the meeting transcript below, create a concise follow-up. Separate: 1) decisions made, 2) action items with owner and deadline only when explicitly stated, 3) unresolved questions, 4) risks or blockers, and 5) what should be revisited next meeting. Do not invent commitments. End with a five-line executive summary.

Human checkpoint: Confirm consent, names, deadlines, decisions, and any sensitive information before distribution.

2. Scheduling & Calendar Coordination Agent

Purpose: Reduce the email ping-pong involved in arranging meetings and protect preferred working hours.

Best for: Sales calls, interviews, vendor meetings, team coordination, recurring appointments.

Workflow

- Define working hours, meeting length, buffers, time-zone rules, and unavailable periods.
- Connect only the calendar/email permissions required by the tool.
- Use the agent to suggest or book times based on explicit rules.
- Require confirmation for high-stakes or external meetings until the system proves reliable.
- Audit bookings periodically for conflicts and unintended permissions.

COPY-READY PROMPT

Act as my scheduling coordinator. I need a [LENGTH] meeting with [PERSON/ROLE]. My acceptable days/times are [WINDOWS], my time zone is [ZONE], and I require [BUFFER] between meetings. Draft a short scheduling message with three options and a fallback request for their availability.

Human checkpoint: A calendar action is real-world execution. Keep confirmation in the loop until you trust the rules and permissions.

3. Avatar-Assisted Content Production

Purpose: Produce recurring video content without needing to record every piece from scratch.

Best for: Training clips, explainers, updates, multilingual versions, social video, internal communication.

Workflow

- Create or select an avatar/voice only with proper rights and consent.
- Write a script for spoken delivery rather than written prose.
- Generate a draft and inspect lip-sync, pronunciation, pacing, tone, and visual artifacts.
- Add B-roll, captions, branding, and human editing.
- Disclose synthetic media when appropriate and avoid deceptive impersonation.

COPY-READY PROMPT

Rewrite this draft as a natural 45-second spoken video script for [AUDIENCE]. Open with a clear hook, use short conversational sentences, mark natural pauses, avoid hype, and finish with one simple call to action. Preserve all factual claims exactly unless I provide evidence for changes.

Human checkpoint: Synthetic likeness and voice require explicit permission, careful disclosure, and human review.

4. Recruiting & Onboarding Knowledge Assistant

Purpose: Give new team members a reliable first place to ask questions about processes, expectations, tools, and policies.

Best for: Small businesses, schools, publishing teams, agencies, volunteer organizations, recurring contractors.

Workflow

- Collect current SOPs, checklists, role descriptions, walkthroughs, FAQs, and policies.
- Remove outdated or conflicting material before loading it into the assistant.
- Instruct the assistant to cite the internal source and admit when an answer is not documented.
- Give new hires a clear escalation path to a human.
- Review unanswered questions to identify missing SOPs.

COPY-READY PROMPT

You are our onboarding assistant. Answer only from the supplied company materials. For every answer, name the source document or section you relied on. If the answer is not supported, say "This is not documented yet" and tell the employee who should confirm it. Never invent company policy.

Human checkpoint: An onboarding assistant should reduce repetitive questions, not become an unofficial policy-maker.

5. Research & Video Learning Assistant

Purpose: Turn long videos, interviews, webinars, articles, and technical material into an interactive learning experience.

Best for: Professional development, research, courses, product education, interviews, conference talks.

Workflow

- Provide the source content or use a tool that can ground answers directly in it.
- Ask for a structured summary before asking interpretive questions.
- Separate what the source says from outside knowledge.
- Ask follow-up questions on unclear concepts.
- Use quizzes or teach-back exercises to test understanding.

COPY-READY PROMPT

Use only the source I provide for the first section. Give me: 1) the five most important ideas, 2) the evidence or examples used, 3) terms I should understand, 4) three questions the source leaves unanswered. Then quiz me with five questions. Clearly label anything you add from outside knowledge.

Human checkpoint: For important research, verify quotations, numbers, dates, and conclusions against the original source.

6. Multi-Model Code Review & Debugging

Purpose: Use independent AI reviews to surface bugs, security concerns, edge cases, and maintainability issues before code ships.

Best for: Software teams, scripts, automation, websites, data processing, technical prototypes.

Workflow

- Give the same code and review criteria to two or more capable models when the change is high-risk.
- Compare disagreements rather than automatically choosing the majority answer.
- Consolidate findings into a ranked action plan.
- Apply changes in small, reviewable patches.
- Run tests and complete a final human code review before deployment.

COPY-READY PROMPT
Review this code as a senior engineer. Focus on correctness, security, performance, maintainability, error handling, and edge cases. Rank findings by severity. For each finding, explain the failure mode, show the smallest safe fix, and name the tests that would prove the fix works. Do not rewrite working code without a reason.

Human checkpoint: AI code is untrusted code until it has been reviewed and tested.

7. Business Operations Analyst

Purpose: Structure messy operating information, explore scenarios, identify trends, and prepare decision-ready summaries.

Best for: KPI reviews, pricing, budgeting, scenario planning, staffing, inventory, project economics.

Workflow

- Define the decision you are trying to make before uploading data.
- Use the minimum necessary data and remove sensitive identifiers when possible.
- Ask AI to state assumptions and calculations.
- Stress-test the conclusion with alternative scenarios.
- Have a qualified person review high-stakes financial, legal, tax, or employment decisions.

COPY-READY PROMPT
Act as an operations analyst. Using the data below, identify major trends, unusual variances, and the three decisions that deserve attention. Show your assumptions, explain calculations in plain language, and create best-case, base-case, and worst-case scenarios. Flag any conclusion that depends on missing or uncertain data.

Human checkpoint: AI can organize analysis; accountable people still own financial and business decisions.

8. On-Brand Design Pipeline

Purpose: Translate brand rules into repeatable creative briefs and image prompts so visual production stays consistent.

Best for: Newsletters, social graphics, book promotions, product images, educational materials, presentations.

Workflow

- Create a short visual style guide: palette, typography, composition, mood, subject rules, and "do not use" list.
- Give AI representative examples and ask it to identify recurring design characteristics.
- Generate a detailed creative brief or image prompt.
- Create several drafts and compare them to the brand rules.
- Human-review text, logos, anatomy, trademarks, and visual consistency before publishing.

COPY-READY PROMPT
Act as a brand art director. Turn this content into an image-generation brief that matches my brand: [BRAND RULES]. Specify subject, composition, camera/viewpoint, lighting, palette, texture, negative space, typography-safe area, and elements to avoid. Give me three distinct concepts that still feel like the same brand.

Human checkpoint: Consistency comes from documented visual rules, not from repeatedly asking for "something similar."

9. Human-in-the-Loop Customer Support

Purpose: Draft fast, consistent support responses grounded in current policies while keeping a person responsible for what is sent.

Best for: Small stores, memberships, education programs, publishing support, service businesses.

Workflow

- Build a clean knowledge base of policies, FAQs, approved examples, and escalation rules.
- Draft responses from that source rather than from general model memory.
- Require the assistant to cite or name the policy it used internally.
- Keep human approval for refunds, complaints, safety issues, legal threats, or unusual cases.
- Add approved corrections back into the knowledge base.

COPY-READY PROMPT
Draft a customer-support reply using only the policies and examples I provide. Be warm, concise, and specific. State what we can do, what we cannot do, and the next step. If the policy does not cover the situation, do not guess - mark it for human escalation.

Human checkpoint: Support automation should improve consistency without hiding uncertainty or removing human accountability.

10. Voice-to-Content Idea Pipeline

Purpose: Capture ideas while they are fresh and turn rough spoken thoughts into organized, usable drafts.

Best for: Authors, creators, executives, teachers, consultants, marketers, people who think better aloud.

Workflow

- Record or dictate ideas naturally without trying to sound polished.
- Transcribe the audio.
- Give AI your audience, tone guide, prior examples, and desired output type.
- Ask it to preserve original ideas while removing repetition and organizing structure.
- Review for voice, accuracy, and originality before saving or publishing.

COPY-READY PROMPT
Turn this raw voice-note transcript into a structured draft for [FORMAT]. Preserve my ideas, examples, and personal voice. Remove filler and repetition, but do not add facts or experiences I did not say. First show the core idea and outline; then produce the polished draft.

Human checkpoint: Do not let cleanup erase the speaker's personality. Keep the raw note until the final draft is approved.

11. Email Triage & Reply Drafting

Purpose: Sort inbox attention, summarize long threads, and prepare replies without surrendering control of communication.

Best for: Busy professionals, customer inquiries, project coordination, recurring requests.

Workflow

- Classify messages by urgency, action required, waiting, reference, or low priority.
- Summarize long threads with decisions and open questions.
- Draft replies in the user's tone.
- Require review before sending, especially for money, commitments, conflict, or sensitive topics.
- Track unresolved threads separately from the inbox.

COPY-READY PROMPT
Summarize this email thread in five bullets: context, decisions, requests made of me, deadlines, and unanswered questions. Then draft a reply in a warm professional tone that addresses every open request without committing to anything I have not explicitly approved.

Human checkpoint: A draft assistant is safer than an autonomous sender for consequential email.

12. Document & Policy Analysis

Purpose: Extract obligations, differences, deadlines, definitions, and action items from long documents.

Best for: Policies, contracts for preliminary review, manuals, vendor terms, school documents, grant requirements.

Workflow

- Use the actual document as the source.
- Ask for section-level citations or page references.
- Separate direct requirements from interpretation.
- Create a checklist of actions and deadlines.
- For legal, financial, medical, or regulatory matters, use qualified professional review.

COPY-READY PROMPT
Analyze this document as a structured reading assistant, not as a lawyer. Extract: key obligations, deadlines, fees, renewal/termination terms, unusual clauses, definitions, and questions I should clarify. Cite the page or section for each item. Clearly distinguish the document's wording from your interpretation.

Human checkpoint: Summarization is not professional advice. High-stakes documents require qualified review.

13. Content Repurposing Engine

Purpose: Turn one strong source asset into multiple platform-specific pieces without making them all sound identical.

Best for: Books, newsletters, podcasts, videos, webinars, articles, presentations.

Workflow

- Choose one authoritative source asset.
- Extract the strongest ideas, examples, stories, and quotable concepts.
- Map each idea to the platform where it fits best.
- Rewrite natively for each format instead of simply shortening the same text.
- Track which derivative content came from which source.

COPY-READY PROMPT
Repurpose the source below into: 1) one short video script, 2) one 7-slide carousel outline, 3) one email, 4) three social posts, and 5) one FAQ. Keep the core facts consistent, but make each format feel native to its platform. Do not invent statistics, testimonials, or claims.

Human checkpoint: Repurposing should extend a good idea, not multiply an unverified claim.

14. Publishing & Metadata Assistant

Purpose: Prepare consistent book metadata and publishing assets while reducing repetitive setup work.

Best for: Authors, small publishers, KDP, Payhip, EPUB distribution, audiobook listings.

Workflow

- Create a master metadata record for each title.
- Generate platform-specific descriptions from that approved record.
- Check title, subtitle, author, series, ISBN, page count, age range, and format for consistency.
- Use AI to draft keywords and categories, then verify them against the platform's current rules.
- Run a final preflight before submission.

COPY-READY PROMPT
Using the approved book information below, create a publishing metadata pack with: title, subtitle, short description, long description, audience, age/grade range, seven keyword phrases, category suggestions, author bio, back-cover blurb, and a consistency checklist. Do not change factual book details unless I approve the change.

Human checkpoint: Metadata must match the actual book and the current platform requirements.

15. Product Listing & Storefront Assistant

Purpose: Create clear, consistent product pages across digital storefronts without rewriting everything from scratch.

Best for: Printable products, courses, coloring books, workbooks, templates, digital downloads.

Workflow

- Maintain an approved product facts sheet.
- Generate store-specific copy while preserving page count, format, audience, licensing, and delivery details.
- Create benefit-focused bullets without exaggerated outcomes.
- Prepare SEO title/description and image-text suggestions.
- Review pricing, refund, license, and file-delivery language before publishing.

COPY-READY PROMPT
Create a complete product listing from this approved facts sheet. Include a clear title, 1-sentence hook, full description, What's Inside, ideal audience, format/delivery details, personal-use notice if relevant, SEO title, SEO description, and 12 tags. Do not invent features or guarantees.

Human checkpoint: Good product copy clarifies value; it should not create claims the product cannot support.

16. Social Content Planning System

Purpose: Turn business goals and content pillars into a balanced publishing calendar rather than chasing random trends.

Best for: Creators, authors, local businesses, educators, service providers.

Workflow

- Define the audience, offer, brand voice, and 3-5 content pillars.
- Choose a realistic posting cadence.
- Balance education, proof, story, community, and promotion.
- Generate ideas with hooks, format, purpose, and CTA.
- Review actual performance monthly and update the plan.

COPY-READY PROMPT
Build a 30-day content plan for [BRAND] serving [AUDIENCE]. Use these content pillars: [PILLARS]. For each post give the format, hook, core idea, audience value, CTA, and business purpose. Balance education, story, community, authority, and promotion. Do not promise virality.

Human checkpoint: A content calendar is a hypothesis. Performance data should shape the next version.

17. Public Market & Competitor Research

Purpose: Collect public evidence about competitors, customer language, positioning, offers, and market patterns.

Best for: Product planning, positioning, launches, pricing research, content strategy.

Workflow

- Define the research question and decision before searching.
- Use current public sources and record dates.
- Separate observed facts from interpretation.
- Look for patterns across several credible sources rather than one competitor.
- Use findings to sharpen positioning, not to copy protected creative work.

COPY-READY PROMPT
Research the public market for [CATEGORY] to help me decide [DECISION]. Compare 5-10 relevant competitors on audience, positioning, offer structure, price range, key claims, proof signals, and customer objections. Cite current sources. Separate facts, patterns, and your inferences. Finish with opportunities to differentiate without copying competitors.

Human checkpoint: Market research should inform original strategy, not encourage plagiarism or deceptive imitation.

18. Project Planning & Task Breakdown

Purpose: Translate a vague objective into milestones, dependencies, tasks, risks, and a practical next-action list.

Best for: Book launches, website builds, events, product creation, curriculum, marketing campaigns.

Workflow

- Define the desired outcome and deadline.
- List constraints, available people, tools, and dependencies.
- Ask AI for phases and tasks in dependency order.
- Identify risks and decision points.
- Review the plan with the people who will actually do the work.

COPY-READY PROMPT
Turn this goal into an executable project plan: [GOAL]. Include scope, assumptions, milestones, task sequence, dependencies, owners/roles, risks, decisions required, and a "next 7 days" action list. Flag anything that needs clarification rather than inventing it.

Human checkpoint: A project plan is only useful if it reflects real capacity, dependencies, and ownership.

19. Quality-Control / Preflight Reviewer

Purpose: Run a systematic final review before publishing, sending, printing, uploading, or delivering work.

Best for: Books, PDFs, websites, emails, product listings, presentations, forms, reports.

Workflow

- Create a checklist specific to the output and platform.
- Have AI review content for consistency, omissions, contradictions, and formatting risks.
- Use software-specific validators for technical requirements.
- Inspect the rendered/real output, not only source text.
- Fix issues and repeat the preflight.

COPY-READY PROMPT
Act as a final preflight reviewer for [OUTPUT/PLATFORM]. Check factual consistency, spelling, headings, page/section order, missing elements, duplicated content, metadata consistency, accessibility/readability, and platform-specific risks. Return a PASS / FIX / VERIFY table. Do not mark PASS when evidence is missing.

Human checkpoint: AI review complements - but does not replace - technical validators and visual inspection.

20. Personal Knowledge Base & Creator Archive

Purpose: Turn scattered notes, files, decisions, prompts, and project history into reusable institutional memory.

Best for: Creators with many projects, small teams, research libraries, publishing archives, long-running brands.

Workflow

- Choose a simple folder/taxonomy and naming convention.
- Save final decisions separately from raw drafts.
- Tag reusable prompts, templates, brand rules, and lessons learned.
- Use AI to summarize and retrieve information from the archive.
- Periodically remove duplicates and mark outdated guidance.

COPY-READY PROMPT

Help me turn these project notes into a reusable knowledge record. Extract: final decisions, standards to reuse, unresolved questions, reusable prompts/templates, important files, lessons learned, and next steps. Clearly separate approved standards from ideas that were only discussed.

Human checkpoint: An archive becomes valuable when it distinguishes final decisions from abandoned experiments.

Choosing What to Automate

A task is a strong automation candidate when it is frequent, rule-based, time-consuming, and easy to verify. A task is a weak automation candidate when it is rare, highly ambiguous, emotionally sensitive, legally consequential, or difficult to reverse.

Good First Candidates

- Summaries and first drafts
- Formatting and restructuring
- Routine classification and tagging
- Research organization
- Checklist generation
- Transcription cleanup
- Content repurposing
- Recurring reporting

Keep Strong Human Control

- Hiring and firing decisions
- Legal, tax, medical, or financial judgments
- Public statements during crises
- Payments, refunds, or irreversible transactions
- Sensitive customer disputes

- Final creative approval
- Anything involving identity, consent, or reputation

The 30-Day AI Workflow Adoption Plan

Week 1 - Find the Friction

- Write down repetitive tasks that consume time every week.
- Estimate time spent and frequency.
- Choose one low-risk task with a clear definition of "done."

Week 2 - Build the Smallest Useful Version

- Use the Master AI Workflow Formula.
- Keep a human approval checkpoint.
- Test with real examples and record failures.

Week 3 - Standardize

- Write the prompt/instructions as a reusable template.
- Document inputs, output format, and quality rules.
- Create a short checklist for human review.

Week 4 - Measure and Decide

- Compare time saved against correction time.
- Measure quality, consistency, and error rate.
- Keep, revise, or remove the workflow based on evidence.

AI Workflow Scorecard

Before scaling a workflow, score each area from 1 (weak) to 5 (strong):

- Time saved
- Output quality
- Ease of verification
- Privacy/safety fit
- Consistency
- Cost effectiveness
- Ease of training another person to use it
- Ability to recover when it fails

A workflow that saves time but creates hidden risk is not a good workflow. The best systems are useful, understandable, reviewable, and reversible.

The Prompt Bible Principle

Do not ask, "What can AI do?" Ask, "Which part of this real workflow can AI improve without removing the human judgment that matters?"

Start small: define the job, use clear source material, keep a human checkpoint, measure the result, and scale only what works.

PART X

PRACTICE LAB & WORKSHEETS

Turn Prompt Knowledge Into Repeatable Skill

This section turns the reference material in The Prompt Bible into guided practice. The goal is not to fill pages for the sake of having a workbook. Each exercise is included because it helps the reader make a better decision, build a stronger prompt, test an idea, or create a reusable system.

How to Use the Practice Lab

1. Read the related chapter or reference first.
2. Study the worked example and notice what changed between the weak and improved versions.
3. Complete the worksheet using a real project whenever possible.
4. Run the prompt, review the output, and record what worked or failed.
5. Save the final version only after it performs reliably.

THE PRACTICE LAB RULE

Do not judge a prompt only by how impressive it sounds. Judge it by whether it consistently produces a useful result for the real task.

A clear, repeatable prompt is more valuable than a complicated prompt that works only once.

Prompt Engineering Lab

Related reference: Part II - Prompt Engineering. Use these pages to practise moving from vague requests to clear, reusable instructions.

Worked Example: From Vague to Production-Ready

Version 1 - Weak Prompt

WEAK PROMPT

Write a product description for my workbook.

What Is Missing?

- Who the product is for
- What the workbook contains
- Where the description will be used
- Desired tone
- Length and structure
- Claims to avoid
- Required call-to-action

Version 2 - Better Prompt

BETTER PROMPT

Write a product description for a 112-page cursive handwriting workbook for children ages 7-11. The description is for an online product page. Use a warm, professional tone and explain what learners practise.

Version 3 - Production Prompt

PRODUCTION PROMPT

Act as an educational-product copywriter. Write a polished product description for a 112-page cursive handwriting workbook for ages 7-11 and Grades 2-5. Emphasize the learning progression from basic strokes to letters, joins, words, sentences, paragraphs, practical writing, and signatures. Use clear parent-friendly language, avoid guaranteed learning claims, include a short "What's Inside" section, and finish with a natural call-to-action. Keep the main description under 350 words.

Why Version 3 Is Stronger

- Role defines the perspective.
- Audience and product facts reduce guesswork.
- Scope tells the model what to emphasize.
- Constraints prevent exaggerated claims.
- Format instructions shape a usable deliverable.
- Length keeps the output appropriate for the platform.

Worksheet: Build Your Own Professional Prompt

PROMPT BUILDER	
The task	What exactly do you want AI to do? -- ---
Role / perspective	What expertise or viewpoint should guide the answer? -- ---
Audience	Who will read, use, buy, or act on the result? -- ---
Context	What does AI need to know before starting? -- --- -- ---
Inputs / source material	What files, notes, facts, examples, or data should be used? -- --- -- ---
Constraints	What must be included, excluded, verified, or avoided? -- --- -- ---
Output format	Paragraphs, table, checklist, script, JSON, worksheet, etc. -- ---
Quality standard	What would make the result genuinely useful? -- ---

My Final Prompt

Worksheet: Prompt Upgrade Clinic

Choose one prompt you use often. Improve it deliberately rather than adding random detail.

PROMPT UPGRADE WORKSHEET	
Original prompt	
Problem with it	☐ Too vague ☐ Wrong tone ☐ Missing context ☐ Weak format ☐ Unverified claims ☐ Other: ______
What AI is guessing	
Context to add	
Constraints to add	
Output format	
Improved prompt	
Result after testing	

Worksheet: Prompt Testing Tracker

A good prompt should survive more than one test. Use the same prompt with several realistic inputs and compare the results.

Test	Input Used	What Worked	What Failed	Revision Needed
1				
2				
3				
4				
5				

Final revision to keep: ____

____

____

____

Prompt Quality Scorecard

Score Your Prompt Before Saving It

Criterion	1-2 Needs Work	3-4 Strong	5 Excellent
Clear task	☐	☐	☐
Enough context	☐	☐	☐
Correct audience	☐	☐	☐
Useful constraints	☐	☐	☐
Defined output format	☐	☐	☐
Appropriate tone	☐	☐	☐
Source handling	☐	☐	☐
No contradictions	☐	☐	☐
Easy to verify	☐	☐	☐
Reusable with new inputs	☐	☐	☐

Total score: ______ / 50

If the prompt scores below 35, revise it before adding it to your permanent prompt library.

Command Stack Builder

BUILD A REUSABLE COMMAND STACK	
Primary role	/teacher /copywriter /critic /research /strategy /other: ______
Tone	/warm /professional /human /direct /friendly /other: ______
Depth	/brief /deep /simple /expert /stepbystep
Output	/table /bullets /checklist /script /finalonly
Quality check	/critic /verify /proofread /factcheck
My stack	____ ___ ____ ___ ____ ___

AI Image & Video Prompt Lab

Related references: Part VI - Image Creation and the 30 AI Video Visual Style Prompts. These worksheets help readers separate subject, composition, lighting, camera, style, motion, and continuity instead of throwing everything into one sentence.

Worked Example: Basic Image Prompt

BASIC PROMPT
A fox reading a book in a forest.

Production-Ready Version

IMPROVED IMAGE PROMPT
A small red fox sits beneath an old oak tree reading an open book, surrounded by ferns and soft woodland flowers. Golden-hour sunlight filters through the leaves from camera left, creating warm rim light around the fox. Medium-wide composition at eye level, shallow depth of field, natural textures, detailed fur, calm storybook mood, balanced negative space above the subject, no text, no extra limbs, consistent anatomy.

What Changed?

- Subject and action became specific.
- Environment gained usable detail.
- Lighting received direction and mood.
- Composition and camera angle were defined.
- Quality and consistency constraints were added.

Worksheet: Visual Prompt Builder

IMAGE PROMPT BLUEPRINT	
Subject	Who or what is the focal point? ____________________
Action / pose	What is happening? ____________________
Environment	Where is the scene? What matters in the background? ____________________ ____________________
Composition	Close-up, medium, wide, overhead, symmetrical, rule of thirds? ____________________
Lighting	Time of day, direction, softness, contrast, practical light sources. ____________________ ____________________
Camera / lens	Angle, lens feel, depth of field, distance. ____________________
Visual style	Photoreal, watercolor, paper craft, low-poly, etc. ____________________
Color / grading	Warm, muted, monochrome, pastel, cinematic, etc. ____________________
Avoid	Unwanted text, extra objects, distortion, clutter, etc. ____________________

Final Image Prompt

____
____
____
____
____

Worksheet: Style Comparison Test

Keep the subject and composition constant. Change only the style. This isolates what the style instruction is actually doing.

ONE VARIABLE AT A TIME	
Base scene	____ ___ ____ ___ ____ ___
Style A	Name: ____________________ Result notes: ____ ___ ____ ___
Style B	Name: ____________________ Result notes: ____ ___ ____ ___
Style C	Name: ____________________ Result notes: ____ ___ ____ ___
Best choice	Why? ____ ___ ____ ___ ____ ___
What I learned	____ ___ ____ ___ ____ ___

Worksheet: Character Consistency Sheet

Use this page before generating a character across many scenes. The goal is to describe what must remain stable and what is allowed to change.

CHARACTER LOCK SHEET	
Character name	____
Species / age / type	____ ____
Face / key features	____ ____
Body proportions	____
Clothing / accessories	____ ____
Signature colors	____
Personality cues	____
Must NEVER change	____ ____
Can vary by scene	____ ____

Worksheet: AI Video Scene Builder

VIDEO SHOT BLUEPRINT	
Scene objective	What must the viewer understand or feel by the end? --- ---
Opening frame	Describe the exact starting image. --- --- --- ---
Subject action	One clear action or movement. --- ---
Camera movement	Static, push-in, pan, orbit, dolly, crane, handheld, etc. --- ---
Environment motion	Leaves, smoke, water, crowds, fabric, light, etc. --- ---
Lighting	What changes or remains stable? --- ---
Ending frame	Where should the shot land? --- --- --- ---
Continuity locks	Character, wardrobe, props, direction, time of day. --- --- --- ---
Avoid	Fast motion, warping, jump cuts, unwanted objects, etc. --- ---

Worksheet: Shot & Motion Planner

Shot	Duration	Framing	Subject Motion	Camera Motion	Transition
1	____ sec				
2	____ sec				
3	____ sec				
4	____ sec				
5	____ sec				
6	____ sec				
7	____ sec				
8	____ sec				

Continuity notes: ____
____
____
____

Marketing & Social Media Practice Lab

Related reference: Part V - Instagram Growth & Audit Toolkit. These pages turn the audit prompts into a repeatable content and conversion system.

Worked Example: Instagram Profile Diagnosis

Observed Profile

- Bio says only "Author | Creator."
- Pinned posts are old announcements.
- Recent Reels show products but rarely explain who they are for.
- Calls-to-action alternate randomly between "link in bio," "buy now," and no CTA.

Weak Advice

WEAK OUTPUT

Post more Reels, use better hashtags, and improve your bio.

Useful Diagnosis

STRONGER OUTPUT

The primary issue is not posting frequency; it is positioning clarity. Rewrite the bio to state the audience and core value, replace at least one pinned post with a "Start Here" post, create three content pillars tied to the product categories, and use one consistent next-step CTA for each campaign. Measure profile visits-to-link clicks before changing posting frequency.

Lesson

Good AI marketing analysis should connect an observation to a reason, an action, and a measurement. Generic advice is not a strategy.

Worksheet: Content Pillar Builder

CONTENT PILLAR MAP	
Audience	Who are you trying to help or attract? ____ ____
Core promise	What should your account become known for? ____ ____
Pillar 1	Topic: _________ Purpose: _________ Example posts: ____ ____
Pillar 2	Topic: _________ Purpose: _________ Example posts: ____ ____
Pillar 3	Topic: _________ Purpose: _________ Example posts: ____ ____
Optional Pillar 4	Topic: _________ Purpose: _________ Example posts: ____ ____
Stop / reduce	What content is confusing, repetitive, or off-brand? ____ ____ ____

Worksheet: 7-Day Content Planner

Day	Format	Pillar	Hook	Value / Story	CTA
Mon					
Tue					
Wed					
Thu					
Fri					
Sat					
Sun					

Balance Check

Education ___ Story ___ Proof ___ Community ___ Promotion ___ Other ___

Worksheet: Reel Optimizer

REEL REVIEW	
Reel goal	Reach / educate / entertain / build trust / sell / other: ______
First 3 seconds	What does the viewer see and hear immediately? ____ ___ ____ ___
Hook	Exact opening line or on-screen text. ____ ___ ____ ___
Viewer payoff	What do they gain by staying? ____ ___ ____ ___
Pacing risk	Where might attention drop? ____ ___ ____ ___
Visual clarity	Can the story be understood without sound? ____ ___ ____ ___
Caption role	Add context / reinforce value / tell story / convert. ____ ___ ____ ___
CTA	One clear next step. ____ ___ ____ ___
One improvement	If I could change only one thing, it would be: ____ ___ ____ ___

Worksheet: Hook Bank Builder

Build hooks around tension, curiosity, specificity, transformation, or relevance - not empty clickbait.

Hook Type	Formula	My Version
Problem	If you struggle with [problem], try this...	
Mistake	The mistake I kept making with [topic]...	
Specific result	Here are 3 ways to [result] without [pain]...	
Contrarian	You may not need more [common advice]. You may need...	
Behind the scenes	Here is exactly how I [process]...	
Before / after	I changed one thing in [process], and here is what happened...	
Question	What would you do if [specific scenario]?	
List	5 things I wish I knew before [task]...	

Worksheet: CTA Builder

A call-to-action should match the stage of the relationship. Do not ask every viewer to buy immediately.

CALL-TO-ACTION LADDER	
Awareness CTA	Save this / share it / follow for _____ My version: ____ ____
Conversation CTA	Comment _____ / tell me _____ / vote _____ My version: ____ ____
Consideration CTA	See the full guide / compare options / read more My version: ____ ____
Conversion CTA	Shop / download / book / subscribe / join My version: ____ ____
After-purchase CTA	Use / review / share / continue learning My version: ____ ____

Monthly Instagram Review Worksheet

MONTHLY CONTENT REVIEW	
What grew	Reach, profile visits, saves, shares, link clicks, sales - what actually improved? ______ ______ ______
Top 3 posts	1. ______ Why it worked: ______ 2. ______ Why it worked: ______ 3. ______ Why it worked: ______
Weakest pattern	What repeatedly underperformed? ______ ______ ______
Audience signals	Questions, comments, DMs, search terms, objections. ______ ______ ______
What to repeat	______ ______ ______
What to stop	______ ______ ______
One experiment next month	______ ______

AI Workflow Design Lab

Related reference: Part VII - The AI-Powered Workplace. These pages help readers decide where AI belongs in a workflow and where human judgment must remain.

Worked Example: One Source to Many Assets

The Real Job

A creator publishes one useful 1,500-word article and wants to turn it into a newsletter, Reel script, carousel, short post, and sales email without making every piece sound copied.

Weak Workflow

WEAK WORKFLOW

Paste article into AI five times and ask it to shorten it for each platform.

Better Workflow

1. Extract the article's strongest ideas, examples, claims, stories, and takeaways.
2. Choose which idea best fits each platform rather than forcing every idea everywhere.
3. Define the native format and audience expectation for each platform.
4. Generate each derivative asset from the source notes, not by repeatedly shrinking the same copy.
5. Human-review tone, facts, and calls-to-action before publishing.
6. Record which source asset produced which derivatives for future reuse.

WORKFLOW PROMPT

Act as a content repurposing editor. Use the attached source as the only factual basis. First extract 8-12 distinct ideas, examples, or lessons. Then map the best ideas to: newsletter, 30-second Reel, 7-slide carousel, short social post, and sales email. Do not simply summarize the same points five times. For each asset, state the audience goal, hook, content angle, CTA, and any fact that must be verified before publishing.

Worksheet: Workflow Design Canvas

AI WORKFLOW CANVAS	
Real outcome	What finished result matters?
Trigger / starting point	What begins the workflow?
Inputs	Files, emails, forms, data, notes, links, etc.
Human-only decisions	What requires judgment, consent, approval, or accountability?
AI-assisted steps	Which parts can AI draft, classify, summarize, compare, or transform?
Tools / systems	What tools are used, and why?
Output	What is produced? In what format?
Verification	How will errors be detected?
Fallback	What happens when AI fails or data is missing?

Worksheet: Automation Candidate Scorecard

Score each factor from 1 (low) to 5 (high). High-value automation candidates are frequent, repetitive, verifiable, and low-risk.

Factor	Score 1-5	Notes
Frequency	____	
Time consumed	____	
Rule-based nature	____	
Input consistency	____	
Ease of verification	____	
Cost of a small error	____	
Privacy fit	____	
Need for human judgment	____	
Ease of rollback	____	
Expected time saved	____	

Decision: ☐ Automate/assist now ☐ Pilot first ☐ Keep mostly human ☐ Do not automate

Worksheet: Human Checkpoint Map

Insert human approval where the consequences of a mistake become meaningful.

Step	AI Does	Human Checks	Risk if Wrong	Approval Needed?
1				☐ Yes ☐ No
2				☐ Yes ☐ No
3				☐ Yes ☐ No
4				☐ Yes ☐ No
5				☐ Yes ☐ No
6				☐ Yes ☐ No
7				☐ Yes ☐ No

Final accountable person: ______________________________

Worksheet: AI Workflow Test Log

Test Date	Example Input	Time Saved	Error / Friction	Change for Next Test

Pilot Decision

☐ Keep as-is ☐ Revise prompt ☐ Change tool ☐ Add human checkpoint ☐ Stop using workflow

30-Day Workflow Adoption Tracker

Week 1 - Find the Friction

Task I want to improve: ____

____

Current time spent: _________ Frequency: _________ Biggest pain point:

____

____

Week 2 - Build the Smallest Useful Version

AI-assisted step: ____

____

Human checkpoint: ____

____

Success definition: ____

____

Week 3 - Standardize

Reusable prompt / procedure: ____

____

____

____

Checklist for review: ____

____

____

Week 4 - Measure

Time saved: ______ Corrections required: ______ Quality score: ______ / 5

Decision for next month: ____

____

____

Mini Case Studies: Putting the System Together

These examples show how several Prompt Bible techniques can work together inside a real project. They are deliberately practical rather than idealized.

Case Study 1 - Author / Publisher: Launching a Workbook

1. Create one approved facts sheet: title, subtitle, page count, audience, format, benefits, disclaimers, price, and delivery details.
2. Use a metadata prompt to draft Amazon and storefront descriptions from the same facts.
3. Use the Image Prompt Builder to develop cover concepts.
4. Use the Social Content Planner to create launch posts from the approved positioning.
5. Run the Preflight Reviewer before upload.
6. Save final metadata and prompts in the project archive.

CASE STUDY PROMPT

Use the attached approved product facts as the only factual source. Create: (1) a 250-word product description, (2) a 100-word short description, (3) seven search-keyword phrases, (4) five social hooks, and (5) a final consistency checklist. Flag any missing fact instead of inventing it.

Practice

Which fact sheet would you need before running this workflow?

____

____

____

____

Case Study 2 - Teacher: Creating a Lesson & Practice Pack

1. Define grade, subject, learning objective, prior knowledge, time available, and assessment goal.
2. Generate the lesson outline first - not the worksheet first.
3. Create examples at the correct difficulty level.
4. Generate practice items, then separately generate and verify the answer key.
5. Check accessibility, ambiguity, and age-appropriate language.
6. Pilot with a small sample before producing a large pack.

CASE STUDY PROMPT

Act as an experienced elementary educator. Create a 45-minute lesson for Grade 4 on [TOPIC]. Include learning objective, warm-up, explicit instruction, guided practice, independent practice, exit ticket, differentiation, and a separate answer key. Keep all examples within the stated skill level. Mark any item that could reasonably have more than one correct answer.

Practice

What information would change the lesson most? ____

____

____

____

Case Study 3 - Creator: One Book, One Month of Content

1. Extract themes, characters, lessons, questions, behind-the-scenes material, and product benefits from the source book.
2. Choose 3-5 content pillars that support the audience and product.
3. Map ideas across Reels, carousels, stories, still posts, and email.
4. Write platform-native hooks rather than copying one caption everywhere.
5. Track saves, shares, profile visits, clicks, and sales separately.
6. Use the monthly review worksheet to decide what to repeat.

CASE STUDY PROMPT

Using the attached book and approved product details, create a 30-day content bank organized by 4 content pillars. For each idea include format, hook, audience value, CTA, and the source page/chapter it came from. Avoid revealing major spoilers unless explicitly approved.

Practice

What four content pillars would support your current project?

____

____

____

____

____

Case Study 4 - Small Business: Customer Support Assistant

1. Build an approved FAQ and policy source.
2. Classify incoming questions by topic and urgency.
3. Draft replies grounded only in approved policy.
4. Escalate refunds, disputes, legal threats, identity issues, and unusual cases to a human.
5. Human-review before sending during the pilot period.
6. Add recurring unanswered questions to the knowledge base.

CASE STUDY PROMPT

Draft a customer-support reply using only the attached policies and order facts. Be warm, concise, and specific. If the answer is not supported by the source, say "Human review required" and list exactly what information is missing. Do not invent refund eligibility, shipping dates, or policy exceptions.

Practice

Which support situations should never be auto-sent in your business?

____

____

____

____

____

Universal Creator Templates

Use these pages across projects. They are deliberately tool-neutral so they remain useful even when specific AI products change.

Worksheet: AI Tool Evaluation Sheet

TOOL EVALUATION	
Tool / service	Name: ____________________ Date reviewed: ____________________
Job to be done	What exact problem are you evaluating it for? ____
Strengths	____ ____
Weaknesses	____ ____
Privacy / data questions	____ ____
Cost / limits	____
Export / ownership	____
Learning curve	____
Replacement risk	Could the workflow survive if this tool disappeared? ____
Decision	☐ Adopt ☐ Pilot ☐ Watch ☐ Reject Reason: ____

Worksheet: Source & Evidence Checklist

Use when a prompt depends on research, uploaded files, factual claims, or current information.

- ☐ I identified which sources the answer should use.
- ☐ I separated source-derived facts from assumptions or outside knowledge.
- ☐ I checked dates for time-sensitive information.
- ☐ I verified quotes and statistics against the original source.
- ☐ I recorded uncertainty rather than hiding it.
- ☐ I checked whether the source is primary, secondary, promotional, or opinion.
- ☐ I avoided copying copyrighted material beyond what is necessary.
- ☐ I can explain why I trust the final answer.

Source Log

Source	Date	What It Supports	Confidence / Notes

Worksheet: Saved Prompt Card

PERMANENT PROMPT LIBRARY CARD	
Prompt name	______________________________
Best use	When should this prompt be used? ______________________________ ___ ______________________________ ___
Required inputs	What must be supplied each time? ______________________________ ___ ______________________________ ___ ______________________________ ___
The prompt	______________________________ ___ ______________________________ ___ ______________________________ ___ ______________________________ ___ ______________________________ ___ ______________________________ ___ ______________________________ ___ ______________________________ ___ ______________________________ ___
Output standard	______________________________ ___ ______________________________ ___ ______________________________ ___
Human review checklist	______________________________ ___ ______________________________ ___ ______________________________ ___ ______________________________ ___

Version / date	Version: ______ Last tested: ______ Owner: ______

Worksheet: Project Prompt Brief

PROJECT CONTEXT SHEET	
Project	Name / client / product / campaign: ____
Primary goal	____
Audience	____
Approved facts	____ ____
Brand / voice	____ ____
Do not change	____ ____
Do not claim	____ ____
Output formats needed	____ ____
Source files	____ ____
Final approver	____

Worksheet: AI Experiment & Lessons Log

Experiment	What I Changed	Result	Lesson	Keep?
				☐ Y ☐ N
				☐ Y ☐ N
				☐ Y ☐ N
				☐ Y ☐ N
				☐ Y ☐ N
				☐ Y ☐ N
				☐ Y ☐ N
				☐ Y ☐ N

Worksheet: Monthly AI Review

MONTHLY AI PRACTICE REVIEW	
Most useful workflow	What saved the most time or improved quality?
Most disappointing use	What looked promising but failed?
Prompt improved	Which prompt got better this month? Why?
Tool worth keeping	
Tool worth dropping	
Risk / privacy issue noticed	
Skill I need to improve	
One experiment next month	

Challenge: The 10-Minute Prompt Makeover

Set a 10-minute timer. Choose one weak prompt from your real work and improve it using the checklist below.

- ☐ Clarify the task.
- ☐ Add audience.
- ☐ Add relevant context.
- ☐ Identify source material.
- ☐ Add constraints.
- ☐ Choose an output format.
- ☐ Define what "good" looks like.
- ☐ Remove contradictions and unnecessary words.

Before

____
____
____
____
____

After

____
____
____
____
____

What Improved Most?

____
____
____

Build Your Personal AI Operating System

The goal of The Prompt Bible is not to make readers dependent on individual prompts. The goal is to help them build a personal system for thinking, creating, testing, and improving with AI.

MY AI OPERATING SYSTEM	
My top 5 recurring tasks	1. ______ 2. ______ 3. ______ 4. ______ 5. ______
My best saved prompts	1. ______ 2. ______ 3. ______ 4. ______ 5. ______
My trusted sources / libraries	____ ___ ____ ___ ____ ___
My human-only decisions	____ ___ ____ ___ ____ ___
My review checklists	____ ___ ____ ___ ____ ___
My current AI tools	____ ___ ____ ___ ____ ___
My monthly review date	___________________________
One skill I am building next	____ ___ ____ ___

Context, Accuracy & Verification Practice Lab

Use this lab to practice diagnosing why an AI result is weak before rewriting the entire prompt.

Concept

Strong AI work depends on more than clever wording. The user must decide what the model needs to know, what evidence it should rely on, what a successful answer looks like, and what must be verified.

Worked Example

Weak request: "Write a great sales page for my book."

Diagnosis: The task is understandable, but the AI does not know the audience, book benefits, proof points, tone, offer, page length, call-to-action, or claims it must avoid.

Improved request: "Write a one-page sales page for [BOOK]. The audience is [AUDIENCE]. Use only the product facts I provide. Emphasize [BENEFITS]. Match this tone: [TONE / EXAMPLE]. Include a headline, short opening, five benefit bullets, what the buyer receives, and one clear CTA. Do not invent reviews, awards, credentials, scarcity, or results. Flag any product detail you need before drafting."

Practice

- Choose one prompt you use repeatedly.
- Run it once without changing anything and save the result.
- Use the Context Advantage to identify what information was missing.
- Use the Example Ladder if style or structure was weak.
- Use the AI Accuracy Ladder if factual grounding was weak.
- Run the TRUST Check on anything you would publish or act on.
- Use the Prompt Improvement Loop to create a second version and compare the two.

Scorecard

- Goal is explicit: 0 1 2
- Useful context is present: 0 1 2
- Source material is appropriate: 0 1 2
- Examples are used when needed: 0 1 2
- Constraints and output format are clear: 0 1 2
- Uncertainty and verification are addressed: 0 1 2
- The result can be reused or refined: 0 1 2

12-14 = Strong and reusable. 8-11 = Useful but improvable. 0-7 = Diagnose the missing ingredient before making the prompt longer.

Reusable Template

TASK: [WHAT I NEED]
GOAL: [WHY IT MATTERS]
BACKGROUND: [CONTEXT]
SOURCE MATERIAL: [FACTS / FILES / DATA]
EXAMPLES: [OPTIONAL PATTERNS]
AUDIENCE: [WHO THIS IS FOR]
CONSTRAINTS: [LIMITS / EXCLUSIONS]
OUTPUT: [FORMAT]
SUCCESS CRITERIA: [WHAT GOOD LOOKS LIKE]
VERIFY: [WHAT MUST BE CHECKED]
FINAL STEP: Review your own result against the success criteria and revise once if needed.

Final Practice Lab Principle

THE PRINCIPLE

The goal is not to use AI everywhere. The goal is to know exactly where it helps, exactly where it does not, and how to stay accountable for the final result.

Three Questions to Carry Forward

1. What work should I systematize because it is repetitive and easy to verify?

____

____

2. What work should remain strongly human because judgment, consent, creativity, or accountability matter?

____

____

3. What is one workflow I will test next - and how will I measure whether it actually helped?

____

____

____

Using These Worksheets

Return to these pages whenever you want to practise a method with a real project. The goal is not to complete every worksheet once; it is to build habits you can reuse.

THE AI PROBLEM SOLVER

A paperback-first decision system for finding the right AI method — without hunting through the whole book.

START HERE: Choose the statement that best matches what you need. Then turn to the Quick Routes page for exact locations in this edition.

CREATE	RESEARCH	SOLVE
Make something new Writing • Images • Video • Content	Find and understand information Sources • Comparison • Synthesis	Fix a problem Diagnose • Decide • Improve
ANALYZE	**PLAN**	**VERIFY**
Understand what you have Documents • Data • Feedback	Turn a goal into steps Projects • Campaigns • Learning	Check what matters Facts • Claims • Sources • Risk

How to use this guide

1. Pick the starting category that best matches your goal.
2. Turn to the Quick Routes page and choose the closest real task.
3. Go to the referenced tool, workflow, worksheet, or Practice Lab and use it with a real project.
4. If the result is weak, use the Prompt Doctor and Critic Panel before starting over.

Example path

I want to promote a new product → MARKETING → Instagram Growth & Audit Toolkit (pp. 55-64) → Marketing Practice Lab (pp. 102-108) → AI Critic Panel (p. 134).

QUICK ROUTES — WHERE SHOULD I GO?

Choose the task that is closest to what you need. Every route below points to material that is in this edition.

WRITING & PROMPTING – books • emails • lessons • scripts • reusable prompts

Use: Shorthand Command Language (pp. 5-43) → Context & Accuracy Systems (pp. 44-46) → Universal Master Prompt Builder (p. 132)

IMAGE & VIDEO – illustrations • covers • scenes • story sequences

Use: Master Video Prompt Formula (p. 66) → Style Directory (p. 67) → 30 Visual Styles (pp. 68-75) → Image & Video Prompt Lab (pp. 96-101)

MARKETING – posts • Reels • campaigns • profile • conversion path

Use: Instagram Growth & Audit Toolkit (pp. 55-64) → Marketing Practice Lab (pp. 102-108)

WORKFLOWS – business • publishing • planning • repeatable processes

Use: The AI-Powered Workplace (pp. 77-89) → AI Workflow Design Lab (pp. 109-114)

RESEARCH & VERIFY – sources • claims • documents • current information

Use: Research & Verification Commands (p. 18) → Context & Accuracy Systems (pp. 44-46) → Source & Evidence Checklist (p. 121) → Verification Lab (p. 128)

FIX & IMPROVE – weak prompts • weak output • quality control

Use: Prompt Quality Scorecard (p. 95) → Prompt Doctor (p. 133) → AI Critic Panel (p. 134)

THE UNIVERSAL MASTER PROMPT BUILDER

One system for building the prompt you actually need.

Level 1 — Quick Builder

MY GOAL	What do I want AI to accomplish? --
MY AUDIENCE	Who is the result for? --
IMPORTANT CONTEXT	What background changes the answer? --
SOURCE MATERIAL	What documents, examples, data, or references should AI use? --
OUTPUT	What should the finished result look like? --
CONSTRAINTS	What must AI include, avoid, preserve, or not assume? --
SUCCESS	How will I know the result is good enough? --
VERIFICATION	What claims, facts, numbers, or decisions must be checked? --

Level 2 — Guided Interview

Use the master instruction below when you want AI to interview you instead of filling in the worksheet yourself.

> Help me build the strongest reusable prompt for my objective. Interview me one question at a time. Do not write the final prompt until you understand my goal, intended audience, relevant context, available source material, constraints, desired output, quality standard, and what needs verification. Adapt each next question to my previous answer. When you have enough information, create: (1) a concise prompt, (2) a detailed master prompt, (3) a reusable template, (4) missing-information warnings, and (5) a short explanation of why the prompt is structured this way.

Level 3 — Save the Winner

Once the prompt works, do not start over next time. Save the proven version, record what inputs change from project to project, and turn the fixed parts into a reusable template or shorthand stack.

THE PROMPT DOCTOR

Diagnose a weak prompt before blaming the AI.

Give the Prompt Doctor both the prompt and the disappointing result. Score each area from 0–10, diagnose the weakest dimensions, then repair only what needs repair.

Goal clarity	____ / 10
Context	____ / 10
Audience	____ / 10
Source material	____ / 10
Constraints	____ / 10
Output specification	____ / 10
Examples	____ / 10
Success criteria	____ / 10
Verification	____ / 10
Reusability	____ / 10
PROMPT HEALTH	**____ / 100**

Prescription

Repair the lowest-scoring dimensions first. Then compare BEFORE → AFTER and explain what changed. A longer prompt is not automatically a better prompt.

Copy-ready diagnostic prompt

Act as a Prompt Doctor. Evaluate my prompt and its result across goal clarity, context, audience, source material, constraints, output specification, examples, success criteria, verification, and reusability. Score each area 0–10. Identify the three biggest causes of failure. Rewrite the prompt with the smallest changes needed to fix those causes. Then explain the repair in plain language. Do not add complexity that does not improve the result.

THE AI CRITIC PANEL

One result. Multiple viewpoints. One final judgment.

CREATOR	Does it fulfill the original intent?
AUDIENCE	Will the intended person understand, value, or act on it?
CRITIC	What is weak, confusing, repetitive, or unconvincing?
SPECIALIST	Does it meet relevant professional standards?
SKEPTIC	Which assumptions may be wrong?
FACT CHECKER	What claims require verification?
EDITOR	What can be removed, clarified, reordered, or strengthened?

THE JUDGE

After the panel reviews the work, synthesize the feedback into four buckets: CRITICAL CHANGES • WORTH CONSIDERING • PERSONAL PREFERENCE • IGNORE. Conflicting advice must be resolved against the original goal and audience, not by majority vote.

Final Rule

Use AI to strengthen your judgment - not replace it.